# LECTIONARY REFLECTIONS

*Commentary for Preachers and Teachers*

CYCLE B

Jill J. Duffield

CSS Publishing Company, Inc.
Lima, Ohio

Lectionary Reflections

# FIRST EDITION
## Copyright © 2020
## by CSS Publishing Co., Inc.

**Library of Congress Cataloging-in-Publication Data: Pending**

Names: Duffield, Jill J., author. Title: Lectionary reflections : commentary for preachers and teachers / Jill Duffield.
Description: First edition I Lima, Ohi0 : CSS Publishing Company, Inc., 2019-
    Contents: Cycle A -- Cycle B
Identifiers: LCCN 2019030223 I ISBN 9780788029790 (cycle A paperback) I ISBN 9780788029806 (cycle A ebook) I ISBN 9780788030123 (cycle B paperback) I ISBN 9780788030130 (cycle B ebook)
Subjects: LCSH: Church year meditations. I Common lectionary (1992).
Classification: LCC BV30 .D74 2019 I DDC 251/.6--dc23 LC

For more information about CSS Publishing Company resources, visit our website at www.csspub.com, email us at csr@csspub.com, or call (800) 241-4056.

e-book:
ISBN-13: 978-0-7880-3013-0
ISBN-10: 0-7880-3013-2

ISBN-13: 978-0-7880-3012-3
ISBN-10: 0-7880-3012-4                    DIGITALLY PRINTED

*To the staff and board of the Presbyterian Outlook in thanksgiving for their commitment to proclaiming the Gospel of Jesus Christ.*

# Contents

## First Sunday of Advent
### Isaiah 64:1-9; 1 Corinthians 1:3-9; Mark 13:24-37

Let's start with the most basic of questions as we kick off Advent this year: Do we really believe that Jesus is coming back?

The wait has been long, over 2,000 years and counting. Additionally, talk of trumpet blasts, clouds, angels, and stars falling from the sky sounds far-fetched. Year after year, I observe the leaves coming and going on my fig tree and on the trees indigenous to my backyard. And, I confess, I do not watch and think: Maybe this is the season Christ comes back, victorious and ready to set things right. Yet, year after year, the Bible smacks me in the forehead with these apocalyptic tales at Advent, texts from the book I affirmed is "the unique and authoritative witness to Jesus Christ in the church universal, and God's Word to me."

How, then, does a contemporary preacher and teacher approach apocalyptic scripture passages with integrity? First, name the strange. Like much of the biblical canon, the readings from Isaiah and Mark this week resound with the unfamiliar. Few among us travel in circles where talk of the end times comes up regularly, although in our current context it may come up more than has been so in the past. (As in: A blue candidate has a chance of winning in a red state and vice versa. Is that a sign of the end times? Some victims of sexual harassment are being believed. Is that a sign of the end times? Total eclipse of the sun, hurricanes and earthquakes. Are those signs of the end times?) Further, more than 2,000 years have passed since Jesus told his followers to keep alert, awake and on the lookout for his return. That's a long time to be vigilant. Drowsiness and eschatological doubtfulness comes with such a long lapse in messianic visitations. Besides, Jesus gave us a mixed message on this front. He said: The signs of my return are visible if you are looking for them (ergo, the fig tree metaphor), *but* no one, not even I, know when the Son of Man will return. So, which is it? We will be able to know, or we can't possibly know?

Even more to the point: So, what? *If* we take Jesus at his word that he will in fact return, what difference does that make for our current living? That's the rub every Advent. We dutifully sing Advent hymns while Christmas music resounds outside our sanctuaries. Mighty gates lift up their heads and watchmen tell of the night, but everyone else shouts of sales, holiday decorations, and gift giving. So why are we looking not just for the birth of baby Jesus, but also the return of the risen and victorious Christ? Why can't we simply enjoy the Christmas parties and pretty lights?

In short, because we need not just Emmanuel, God with us, but the Son of Man, God for the world. We need grace and judgment, mercy and accountability, forgiveness and repentance, love and justice. We need to be claimed *and* transformed. Without a proclamation of the promised parousia, strange and out of cultural place as it no doubt is, Advent slips easily into sentimentality and cheap grace. On the flip side, an emphasis only on the parousia leaves us sitting alone on the judgment seat. We need both God to be with us and on the side of the oppressed and vulnerable. We need the incarnation and the promised parousia. We need one Savior, who is our Lord from birth to death — alpha and omega, past, present and future. We need the judge seated on the right hand of God and the one who takes our place on the cross.

Anticipating both the birth of baby Jesus and the return of the risen Christ calls us to live as Paul admonished in 1 Corinthians 16:13: "Keep alert, stand firm in your faith, be courageous and strong." We must recognize the tension between trusting that the Lord is on the way, but not knowing when he will make his appearance. This makes for lives of daily faithfulness, marked not by fear and anxiety, but by hope and expectation that the Lord is near. That's the "so what" of these clouds, trumpets, falling stars, and fig trees about to sprout. We know whose we are. We know whose future is sure. We know who the potter is and that we are the clay. We know that the world is about to turn and the direction in which it will surely go. We know that we are to turn in that direction too, if we are to be found on the side of the one who comes to set the captives free and bring good news to the poor. That's the "so what" of these end times texts.

John Donahue, in *Harper's Bible Commentary,* wrote that these "synoptic apocalypse" texts gave Christians the "proper posture toward the end of time", and that posture was "vigilance and fidelity (active waiting), not idle speculation." I like that succinct assessment: vigilance and fidelity. We are on the lookout for the current presence and coming judgment of Jesus Christ while living in ways that show our faithfulness to him and our commitment to his commandments. If we can start having this "proper posture" in Advent, perhaps we might be able to sustain it throughout the year.

Advent urges me to consider — not just as a thought experiment, but as a real-life exercise — that if today *is* the day that the Son of Man returns, clouds, power and glory, trumpets, angels, or however he so chooses, what will he find me doing? Will my thoughts, words, and deeds be reflective of his character? Mission? Instructions? Commandments? If not — and let's be honest, we are all going to fall short, and that's where I am counting on grace — what do I need to do differently? And am I willing to at least attempt to do it? Not out of fear, but out of a desire to worship, follow, and please the one who saved me and all of creation.

Keep alert. Keep awake. Don't become complacent or cynical. Don't walk through life drowsy or numb to the present and coming kingdom. The world is about to turn, and we need to be ready to pivot with it, already facing the direction we know God will go, toward love and justice, mercy and accountability, forgiveness and repentance, judgment and grace, *hesed* and vindication for the oppressed: salvation.

This week:

- Do you think about the parousia? If you do, what impact does it have on your understanding of Jesus?
- Would it matter if you knew the day and hour of Jesus' return? Why does Jesus take the time to offer the signs of his return if we really can't know the day and hour? Consider the context of the early Christians and then consider our own context.

- Is the thought of the coming of the Son of Man comforting or scary? Should it be comforting or frightening? Why?
- What is the role of creation in announcing the parousia? How do we, rightly or wrongly, theologically interpret natural disasters, solar eclipses, and the like?
- Note in both the Isaiah text and the one appointed for Mark this week that there is both a cosmic and down-to-earth element in each: tearing open the heavens, potter and clay, darkened sun, and a fig tree. What do you make of this? Can you think of other examples of this?
- Look up the phrase "day of the Lord" in a biblical dictionary. What do you discover? How and where is this used in the Bible?

## Second Sunday of Advent
Isaiah 40:1-11; 2 Peter 3:8-15; Mark 1:1-8

Punctuation matters.

Maybe you've seen those T-shirts and mugs that read: "Let's eat, Grandma" and below it, "Let's eat Grandma" and below that, "Commas save lives." That clever tagline came to mind as I read the texts from Isaiah and Mark for the second Sunday of Advent. In the case of Isaiah, rather than a comma, a colon leapt out as significant. "A voice cried out: 'In the wilderness prepare the way of the Lord....'" Often, I have imagined the voice crying out in the wilderness, with no one there to hear it. But the punctuation of Isaiah, at least in the NRSV, sends a different message. It is almost a directive: 'Go to the wilderness, that's where a way for the Lord must be made.' Mark's version of the prophet's admonition muddied the waters, though. There, a semicolon separates two clauses. The first one: "See, I am sending my messenger ahead of you, who will prepare your way;" the second, "the voice of one crying out in the wilderness: 'Prepare the way of the Lord....'" The colon shows up a word or two later than in Isaiah, so what is the emphasis supposed to be placed upon? The message? The location of the messenger? Perhaps that semicolon and colon serve to show John the Baptist's obedience. Having heard the voice, he went to the wilderness and got to work.

Do such subtleties even matter? So what if the directive is go to the wilderness to prepare the way of the Lord or to go in the wilderness to cry out that the time has arrived to prepare the way of the Lord? Either way, the wilderness plays a role, seemingly the place where the Lord makes his appearance. That'll preach. But still, heading to the wilderness to make a path feels different that standing there, crying out to make one. Perhaps John the Baptist did both. Mark made clear that John was in the wilderness and people from all over were "going out to him." Apparently, his cries were heeded. He may have been in the wilderness, but people were somehow hearing him — people from the whole Judean countryside and all the people of Jerusalem, in fact.

They weren't only hearing, but they were responding, confessing their sins, and being baptized. John, it seemed, was making a way in the wilderness, the wilderness of their lives, in order to for Jesus to find a way to their hearts.

John the Baptist cried out in the wilderness and made a way there, is that also a word for us?

The mistake I have too often made is that crying out in the wilderness is an exercise of futility when, in fact, the wilderness is the place ripe to hear the Word of God, the setting where our true identities are found and formed, the space where transformation begins, for the Israelites, for Jesus, for those who came to John the Baptist and for us. They are found in liminal, in-between, awe-inspiring, and frightening places that jolt us out of the familiar and force us to look hard at who we are and who we wish to be. The wilderness is the place to hear prophets and actually listen what they have to say. The wilderness is also part of us that needs clearing and taming. The placement of the colon is just right, in both texts. Punctuation matters. Colons change lives.

John the Baptist urged us to call others to prepare for Christ's coming, but also to prepare a way within ourselves through confession and repentance, personally and corporately. Go to the wilderness and cry out, recognize the wilderness present within and confess.

Preparing the way for the Lord requires a journey to the wilderness, regardless. Are we willing to go? It would seem that repentance and confession are needed and, in some cases, are happening. There is the spate of powerful men apologizing for sexual misconduct, some with more caveats and qualifications than others. There is the recognition that workplaces and systems have conspired to silence victims of harassment and abuse. Some communities and congregations are wrestling with their racist pasts (and presents). People in various sectors are waking up to the role policy plays in either exploiting or aiding the vulnerable. Is there confession or repentance in the wilderness? Maybe. Are we preparing the way for the Lord? I certainly hope so.

Mark doesn't give us much more than the bare bones description. Mark is like that. We don't get the "What now should we do?" and the follow-up instructions about sharing coats and not exploiting people that Luke delivered. All we get is confession of sins, baptism, a promise that someone far greater is yet to come and will bring with him the Holy Spirit. But confession, baptism, and the promise of the coming Christ gets us pretty far down the road, maybe even out of the wilderness and on our way.

Like Mark, our crying out to make way, repent, confess, and remember your baptism won't go unheard or unheeded. We don't call out in vain when God has given us the task and the message. Nor will our own repentance and confession fail to make ready a place for Jesus to work within us. In a culture replete with people offering equivocal amends and half-hearted admissions, our honest reckoning of sin would be a light to the world, a way in the wilderness through which the transforming power of the Spirit would surely work. Such wilderness wanderings are fraught with wild beasts, unexpected visitors and disorienting landscapes, but they also include manna, water and angels.

I don't really want to face the wilderness, outside or within myself. I understand fully the impetus to make excuses for my behavior and that of the church. I want to stay safely in the privacy of my home. But the voice crying out from the wilderness can't be ignored. It is loud, relentless, and strangely beguiling. Something in me wants to have integrity. Some small part of me longs to be transparent, vulnerable, unburdened, as well as anticipating the judgment of God — because I know the one who came in the wake of the baptismal waters of John is Jesus, the one who came to save sinners, and I don't want anything to impede his arrival.

This week:

- What does repentance mean in our current context? Is it too churchy a word to have meaning for contemporary people? How would you define repentance?
- Have you spent time in the literal wilderness? Metaphorically? Was it a place of transformation or fear, something else?
- What do you need to do to prepare a way for the Lord? What about in your church? Community?

- What does it mean to be baptized by the Holy Spirit?
- What does the weekly prayer of confession mean to you? Is it meaningful to say it together with others? What is the role of silence?
- Where are you called to go raise your voice to prepare the way of the Lord?

**Third Sunday of Advent**
Isaiah 61:1-4, 8-11; 1 Thessalonians 5:16-24; John 1:6-8, 19-28

> "Good news to the oppressed.
> Bind up the brokenhearted.
> Liberty, release, comfort, gladness,
> praise, recompense, righteousness.

The beauty and poetry of the Isaiah text for this week pours over us like the oil of gladness that the prophet promises. Reading each verse rings out like the antithesis to the headlines we hear 24/7. Yemen's civil war threatens to worsen, civilians already without basic resources for survival are trapped as violence rages. Another politician/journalist/actor is named in the #MeToo movement that continues to gain momentum as those long silenced finally speak out. The tsunami of heroin addiction pulls under more victims daily. Investigations into Russia's involvement in the American elections continue. Ordinary people anticipate the impact of actions taken in Washington. Charlottesville grapples with the report detailing what went wrong on August 11-12. North Korea tests missiles and tense relationships between nations get worse.

I could use some good news — for the oppressed, for the brokenhearted, for the fearful, for the vulnerable and captive. I could use some good news for those who mourn and those who huddle in ruined cities and devastated places. The prophet's vision seems too good to be true some days, no matter how badly I want to believe that the Lord who loves justice is on the way. The poetry resounds with beauty while the world all too often wallows in the ugly. The prophet preaches comfort while those in positions of power inure themselves to suffering. The verbs of Isaiah: liberty, comfort, gladness, recompense, and righteousness — are absent from our earthly lexicon. The word of the year, announced last week, was "complicit," after all.

That's why I welcome John the Baptist yet again this Advent season. Normally so out of place during such a festive time of year, John the

Baptist feels strangely right in this year. Speaking truth to power (or at least truth to those with ears to hear), John's proclamation of repentance sounds like the harbinger of good news promised in Isaiah, perhaps now more than ever. But we get an additional word about John the Baptist from John's Gospel and it comes just in time. John the Baptist, we are told, came as a witness to testify to the light. John the Baptist repeats the purpose of his arrival on the scene: to point to Jesus, to let the world know that Jesus is both among the religious authorities even as they interrogate John and coming to bring the promised liberty, comfort and recompense. As the hymn notes: "The world is about to turn." And it depends which side of it you are on, as to whether you welcome this divine pivot. (Rory Cooney, "Canticle of the Turning," Chicago: GIA Publications, 1990)

John the Baptist witnesses to the light. Testifies to the light's presence, a comfort to those huddled in the dark, a threat to those who do not wish to be revealed. The light of Christ has the capacity to warm and enlighten as well as expose and burn. The world is about to turn. The Lord who loves justice and hates robbery and wrongdoing will have the last word, and that word is on the way.

Trusting John's testimony and the prophet's promise, how then are we to respond to Advent in the year when the word of the year is "complicit"?

Rejoice always, pray without ceasing, give thanks in all circumstances, that's what the writer of Thessalonians advises. Don't quench the Spirit. Don't despise the words of the prophets. Test everything. Hold fast to what is good. Abstain from every form of evil. Seems to me a good to-do list if we want to be ready for the word that brings a revealing light – rather than, well, being complicit in the ways of those happy to keep others in the dark.

Testify to the light. That's our role, too. Point to Jesus, among us and on the way. As the relentless roll call of those who are hurt and hurting rings out, be the voice crying out in the wilderness that the days are surely coming when crying and mourning will be no more. Even now, God hears people's moans of pain and we do too. The world is about to turn and as it begins to pivot toward the oppressed, captive, and brokenhearted, we who worship the Lord should already be leaning in that direction. We should be testifying to the light, holding fast to what is good, abstaining from every form of evil, and praying without ceasing. We should be rejoicing and giving thanks, always, in all circumstances. Such behavior unnerves purveyors of darkness, puts them off balance, maybe even prepares them for the Spirit to do a 180° turn on them.

You have no doubt heard the stories of how Nelson Mandela's captors transformed their perception, not only of Mandela, but themselves and their country as well. The accounts of how Dietrich Bonhoeffer carried himself, cared for fellow prisoners and even ministered to his jailers are legend. Testifying to light, during deep darkness, brings the possibility for illumination to all those in proximity. Daily there are people who courageously do similar, not just the Mandelas, the Bonhoeffers, or the Mother Teresa's.

There are the parole officers like Tiffany Whittier, as reported in the *Independent,* whose patient, positive witness allowed light to shine through the racism of one of her clients. So much so, that he had the swastika tattoo removed from his chest. Tiffany is black and Michael Kent, that parolee, white. He said of Tiffany, "She is much more than my parole officer. I would think of her as family." Hold fast to what is good. Abstain from all forms of evil. Do not quench the spirit. (https://www.independent.co.uk/news/world/americas/nazi-swastika-tattoo-remove-friends-black-police-officer-a7968831.html)

There is the husband, a retired physician, who walked with his wife through cancer and her death. He fulfilled his promise to have a home funeral and attended to the details they discussed with their family about her death and burial, handled entirely by those who loved her. Reporter Libby Copeland wrote in *Esquire Magazine* about her time with the couple:

"It was during a conversation in May, about two months before she died, that Kate mused about the beautiful casket Deloy had had a carpenter fashion out of cherry trees blown down by a hurricane. The Oberlins called it "the box" and kept it down in the shed. Kate would not be buried in it, but would be in it while they took her up the mountain. She and Deloy engaged in a long, animated discussion about its merits and limitations. Deloy said she'd fit, but just barely. Kate wondered if she could wear boots as part of her final outfit, or if they'd add too much length. And what would it feel like to climb into the box alive? She kind of wanted to. The Oberlins coped, it seemed to me, by looking straight at what was coming and making it their own. It was the worst kind of adventure, but they were doing it together."[1]

Testifying to the light, giving thanks in all circumstances, and holding fast to what is good is what we should be doing.

Every day there are those who bring good news to the oppressed, love justice and comfort those who mourn in the name of the Lord they follow. Theere are those testifying to the light, pointing to Jesus among us and coming to bind up the brokenhearted. I want to be complicit with them this Advent.

This week:

- What does it mean to pray without ceasing? What might that look like if we think of praying more as a corporate act of the Body of Christ, rather than just as individual Christians?
- The text from Isaiah speaks repeatedly of comfort. How do we comfort one another? When have you experienced comfort?
- John the Baptist was clear about his role: He was a witness who testified to the light. What is our testimony to the light this Advent?
- How do we hold fast to what is good and abstain from every form of evil? How do we keep one another accountable in doing so?

1      (https://www.esquire.com/lifestyle/a12845872/kate-oberlin-home-funeral/?src=longreads&utm_source=Weekly+Longreads+Email&utm_campaign=41aecedb1e-Longreads_Top_5_November_17_2017&utm_medium=email&utm_term=0_bd2ad42066-41aecedb1e-238737117&mc_cid=41aecedb1e&mc_eid=aa3d5134fb)

- Do we really want the world to turn toward the oppressed and suffering? What would that mean for those who are not oppressed and for whom the way the world now functions is beneficial to them?
- Pray each day this week to testify to the light.

## Fourth Sunday of Advent
2 Samuel 7:1-11, 16; Romans 16:25-27; Luke 1:26-38

The annunciation, that angelic announcement to an unsuspecting young woman, comes again this fourth Sunday of Advent. The writer of Luke does not reveal to us what Mary was doing when Gabriel burst onto the scene, called her favored, and told her she would bear a son, the Holy One who would be given the throne of David, no less. No wonder Mary started questioning what sort of greeting this was. The word used in many translations is "discernment." Mary "tried to discern what sort of greeting this might be." This phrase alone could be unpacked for several Sundays. The word "discern" could be translated as "think about," "wonder," "argue," or "discuss." Inserting those different translations changes the tenor of Mary's attitude to this intrusive angel. Mary argued about what sort of greeting this might be. Mary wondered about what sort of greeting this might be. Mary discussed what sort of greeting this might be. Mary's discernment sounds perhaps more pious than Mary arguing, but maybe it helps us to consider Mary as less the artist-rendered holy 'round yon virgin, and instead more like an ordinary person of faith struggling to figure out what God was up to in her life.

Consider for a moment just how disturbing and disruptive Gabriel's message truly was to this young woman on the cusp of marriage. Even in a modern context, an unexpected pregnancy under less than ideal circumstances, while often joyous, always upends envisioned plans for the future. No wonder Gabriel's announcement evoked great distress. Why wouldn't Mary argue with the angel? Certainly other biblical characters did. Moses took issue with God's choice of him to go to Pharaoh saying, "I can't speak well. Surely, there a better choice of candidates exists." Jeremiah said he was unqualified to speak the Word of God, being, after all, only a boy. Amos told the divine that he was no prophet but rather a dresser of sycamore trees. The list goes on. Mary did voice a basic and profound question that echoes through the ages:

"How can this be?" The facts just do not line up. All the laws of nature must be undone for this to take place. Mary, like us, knew the parameters of the realm of possibility, and understood that this prediction could not occur within them.

I like to envision a spunky young Mary discussing this greeting with Gabriel, arguing no less than my teenage daughter does with me, telling the angelic messenger, "Hold up, wait just a minute here, we need to have a talk." While I love the Christmas hymns that depict Mary as peaceful, holy, and content, recognizing a more perplexed, afraid (as angels say "fear not" when the ones they encounter are indeed afraid), distressed, and doubtful, Mary aids ordinary people of faith in their discernment of God's greetings and God's present and coming word.

While we are not Mary, the mother of God, we are no less unworthy to further God's salvation plan for creation. Knowing that all things are possible with God and through God's favor, God's grace obliterates not only our plans, but perhaps even everything we thought within the realm of possibility. How do we hear and heed the divine messengers that surely still announce holy happenings in our lives and in our world?

Trusting that wonder, confusion, discussion, and even argument are necessary when it comes to figuring out what new, godly thing is afoot. This belief opens us to the radical nature of the inbreaking kingdom of heaven and helps us, ultimately, to yield to the new birth God initiates and brings to fruition. Mary's willingness to say, "Behold, I am a servant of the Lord. Let it be with me according to your will," comes only after great distress and much discernment. Her practice of wonder, discussion, thought, and, yes, even argument with the most high, would be repeated as she raised the Son of God, the one destined for the throne of David that led not to a palace, but to the cross. She would sing a song of praise. She would treasure the words of shepherds and ponder much in her heart. She would marvel at what is said about her baby boy. She would know the pain of a sword piercing her heart. I suspect, over and over again, she would need to have her fears assuaged. I suspect, many times throughout the course of her journey with the One who found favor with her, she would be distressed and she would question not only how God would work out God's plans, but why the story unfolded as we know it will.

God's favor, God's grace, disrupts, disturbs and distresses, but only after wrestling with this reality can we begin to accept God's announcement and discover the joy that comes with participating fully in its fulfillment, no whatever it brings. Recognizing Mary as not only the pious virgin, accepting and holy, but as a real person, wanting to be faithful, daily seeking to discern God's Word in the middle of daily living, provides the rest of us with a model to emulate and permission to question in order to be open to the upending grace of God, no matter how impossible it seems.

This week:

- When have you experienced a message from God? How did it come to you? What was its content?
- Have you ever argued with God? Over what? What was the outcome?
- Can you think of other biblical examples of people chosen by God? How did they respond to God's call?
- How have you responded to God's call in your life? How was your response similar to, or unlike, those biblical characters?
- When has God upended your plans or those of your faith community? How were you able to accept the new, strange, unexpected thing God was doing?
- Take a look at images of Mary in art through the ages. What do you notice about how she is depicted? Can you find contemporary images? What do these depictions convey about her? How would you show Mary?

**Nativity of the Lord**
Isaiah 9:2-7; Titus 2:11-14; Luke 2:1-14 (15-20)

Crafting the sermon may be one of the last items left on the *to do* list for Christmas Eve. With all the other things to do and plan, sometimes the homily for this service gets pushed aside until later than we would like. However, I would argue that now is the time for an emphasis on joy, awe, and wonder. Yes, the world still rages with violence, suffering, and upheaval. But for this day, focus on the inbreaking of the holy, the angels' songs, the shepherds' surprise and response, and the ponderings of Mary's heart. The problems of this realm won't disappear, but perhaps going to the manger to worship and departing the sanctuary praising God will enable us to re-enter life with renewed hope and resilience.

Christmas Eve provides the opportunity to remind those gathered that waiting does not last forever. Just days after the darkest day of the year, the light of Christ overwhelms us in the middle of whatever fields we labor. If the warring factions of WWI could pause and remember their humanity and that of their enemies, surely we too can take a break from whatever anger, divisions, and ugliness consume us on Christmas Eve. I discovered on History.com this quote about the Christmas Truce of 1914: "On December 7, 1914, Pope Benedict XV suggested a temporary hiatus of the war for the celebration of Christmas. The warring countries refused to create any official cease-fire, but on Christmas the soldiers in the trenches declared their own unofficial truce." (https://www.history. com/topics/world-war-i/christmas-truce -of-1914#)

I found it moving that the truce was initiated by the soldiers in the trenches. Those most impacted and closest to the horrific realities of war recognized, at least briefly, a reality bigger than war and its causes. Shouldn't we also recognize that the birth of Jesus is bigger than whatever rancor consumes us, our communities, our churches, and our world?

The incarnation of God becoming human for our sakes, should compel us to see the humanity in others. The incarnation, the fully divine becoming fully human, should enable us to see the image of God in everyone. This Christmas Eve, could we take a break, call a truce, hit pause on the barrage of negativity, and bask in the good news of the Messiah's birth?

Hearing repeatedly, and rightly, that we live in a broken world colors the way we see everything and everyone around us. Yes, we are fallen, broken, sinful — but have we forgotten that the Messiah has come to save? The people who walked in darkness have seen a great light; those who lived in a land of deep darkness — on them light has shined — they walked in darkness — *past tense*. God has increased our joy. People rejoice. The shepherds glorify and praise God. All who heard what the shepherds relayed were amazed. Lost in wonder, joy, and praise. How about a little of that this Christmas Eve?

I run with a small group of women several mornings a week. We meet before dawn and this time of year we end just as the sun comes up. I do not relish the early, cold wake-up call. I delight, though, in seeing the sky turn orange and the geese landing on the pond and, this month, in the Christmas lights guiding us on our way. But more than the unveiling of creation and the festive twinkling on trees and homes, I praise God for the company of these women. We are an eclectic crew, brought together only because we want to run at what some would call an ungodly hour and we need to be held accountable. We need to know people are waiting for us, or we would hit "snooze" and go back to sleep. To pass the time and make the experience pleasant, we talk. The others are all varieties of Christians on the spectrum from active in their churches to lapsed attenders: Baptist, Catholic, and Episcopalian. I can't think of many who've taught me more about living faith daily than these women.

One of my early morning companions sings in her church choir, helps care for her mother who has cancer, and just maxed out her credit card to help keep a family member from being evicted. She prayed with a group at church about this soon-to-lose-her-house family member and she told me as we huffed and puffed up a hill, "I realized God was telling me to be the help I was asking God to give." Another woman, a seventy-year-old who just ran a half-marathon and runs circles around me (even though she's not even five feet tall and I am five feet ten inches), cares for her 92-year-old aunt. Her aunt lives with her and before that, her mother lived with her until her death. This woman sees God everywhere. She is the definition of what it is to be lost in wonder, joy and praise. She runs circles around me spiritually as well as physically. Pennies on the ground are reminders to her of God's presence and provision. A shooting star, she sees as reassurance of God's protection. She takes pictures of the hearts she sees in leaves, rocks, shells, and nuts broken apart by creature or nature. She lives this sentiment of Brother David Steindl-Rast: "Our eyes are opened to that surprise character of the world around us the moment we wake up from taking things for granted" (from "*Gratefulness, the Heart of Prayer*").

This morning she showed me three photos: one of an acorn, another of a shell, and the third of a rock. "What do you see?" she asked, expectantly. I struggled with the first one. "A heart?" I muttered. She looked, "Where?" I pointed to the outline that resembled a heart (a Salvador Dali heart, but a heart nonetheless). "Oh, yes! I see. I saw an angel." She outlines it with her finger. Then I saw it, too. The second one was a heart, as symmetrical as any found on a Valentine's Day card, right there, inside an acorn. The third showed a rock that somehow had the impression of what appeared to be a butterfly. "Amazing, right?" she asked as she beamed. Amazing, I thought. It is amazing that one can see signs of God's presence, goodness, promise, beauty, and love everywhere.

On Christmas Eve, our call is to help others see hearts, stars, angels, and our divine-infused world that often seems bereft of light and love everywhere. Call a truce on fear, enmity, and violence. Revel in the good news of great joy for all people. Heed the choir of the heavenly host. Go and worship the Messiah and leave glorifying and praising God for all that you have seen and heard. And then live out all that has been told to you, every day, trusting that others will meet you in the darkest hour before the dawn, keep you accountable and help you on the way.

## Lectionary Reflections

This week:

- When are you aware of God's presence? Do you see signs of the divine in the midst of the mundane?
- What do you need to leave in order to go and worship the Christ child?
- Why do we need to both recognize the brokenness of the world and its God-proclaimed goodness?
- For what are you praising and glorifying God this Advent and Christmas?
- Pay attention this week to signs of God's love, beauty and goodness. Do you notice any hearts, angels, or stars?
- What is it that God is doing in your life that you are pondering in your heart?

**First Sunday after Christmas Day**

Isaiah 61:10-62:3; Galatians 4:4-7; Luke 2:22-40

Mary and Joseph were law abiding Jews.

Simeon and Anna, too, exhibited faithfulness, obedience, and dutifulness. The characters in this story all followed the rules God set before them. According to the Law of Moses, they presented Jesus at the temple, their firstborn dedicated to the Lord, the prescribed sacrifice given. Simeon was righteous and devout. Anna never stopped worshiping and fasting. (How is that even possible?) The narrative for this first Sunday after Christmas could not get any churchier. And, let's be honest, those gathered for worship the Sunday *after* Christmas are the Marys and Josephs, the Simeons and Annas, of our congregations. The dutiful, faithful folks who show up every time the doors open and stay and clean up afterward. So, admonishing everyone to do what God says — worship, tithe, and so on — well, that could be affirming or, alternately, could be less than revelatory or, even worse, self-congratulatory. Look at us, we're here, we get to see Jesus! (I think I've preached that sermon.)

But what happens when we consider this text in light of those who aren't praying, fasting, patiently waiting, or always in the sanctuary, fellowship hall, church kitchen, or Sunday school classrooms? What does this story have to do with them? Why should they care? What difference does Jesus' presentation at the temple mean to all those getting ready to party into the new year, or hit the after Christmas sales, or head to work at a job that has no regard for Sundays or the sacred? What about for those who went to their annual worship service on Christmas Eve last week, with no intentions of returning until next year's dimly lit and lovely service?

The key is in the text itself, because as churchy as this story seems to be, all that happens inside that temple is for the sake of those oblivious to it in the world. Note what Simeon said when he took up Jesus in his arms and praised God: he had seen salvation, "prepared in the presence

31

of all peoples, a light for the revelation to the Gentiles and for the glory of your people Israel." Simeon, righteous and devout, understood that the Messiah had come for the unrighteous and the unclean, God's people Israel as well as the Gentiles. Anna, in her old age, was less concerned with the state of her own soul than with the redemption of Jerusalem. She was a prophet, after all, and prophets don't work for themselves; they take their orders from God. Their fasting and praying, worshiping and praising, all point away from themselves and toward the one who calls and sends.

No, this story doesn't tell us to feel good about our dutifulness, commend us for showing up as instructed, nor admonish us to go get others to church or temple. This story proclaims, even at this earliest phase of Jesus' life, that the Messiah has come for the sake of the world, the partygoers and service workers, the lapsed faithful and those who've never darkened the door of a holy place, the chosen people of Israel and the Gentiles who still stumble around in the darkness. We would do well to remember that Mary and Joseph, Simeon and Anna embrace a child who will not be held, not even by the cross or a grave. Jesus would soon cause his parents to worry when he tarried in the temple and got left behind. Before long, a sword would pierce his mother's soul because Jesus had come not to stay safely in any sanctuary, but to venture out into the wilderness and then into a world that will have him killed.

Mary and Joseph, Simeon and Anna, came to the temple to worship the God who both created and loved all that is seen and unseen. The salvation they beheld became incarnate for all people. Their devout, dutiful righteousness compelled them to follow the law of Moses, enabled them to see the Messiah, and know they cannot keep him to or for themselves. Do those of us sitting in the pews or standing in the chancel week after week, fasting and praying without ceasing understand this, too?

Every churchy thing we do should compel us out into the world God so loves, proclaiming that salvation, redemption, consolation has come for everyone. We can't expect those who neither know nor care about the law of Moses (never mind the new commandment to love one another) to be at worship this week. We should, however, expect that our having been there changes us, how we see others, the decisions we make, the words we utter and the way we live and move and have our being. Do you think Mary and Joseph, or Simeon and Anna, were ever the same again? Then how can we leave an encounter with the living Lord, shrugging our shoulders and saying, "meh"?

Sometimes I wonder if we expect anything at all when we go to worship. When we put our money in the plate, confess our sin or pass the peace, hear the word read and proclaimed, the benediction pronounced, do we eagerly expect consolation, redemption? Do we expect an encounter with salvation? Do we imagine that what we do inside those spaces has an impact when we walk out the door? Do we have any idea that we have witnessed the light for the revelation of all nations? Annie Dillard's quip about the need to wear crash helmets in worship is often quoted, but rarely heeded. (I wonder what would happen if the ushers did pass some out one Sunday?)

Truth be told, Simeon and Anna, and Mary and Joseph as well, went to temple many times with Jesus nowhere in sight. But they went anyway. They kept going. They were, as my Greek lexicon puts it, "looking forward to the fulfillment of expectation." And darned if their expectations weren't met. What if we went to worship this week, and next, and the next, looking forward to the fulfillment of expectation: the expectation that God is doing a new thing, that Jesus has come to save, that we are united in Christ. Expecting that reconciliation is inevitable, that death and sin have been defeated, that the Holy Spirit speaks to and through us, that when we are gathered Jesus is in the midst of us no less than he was in the temple that day with Mary and Joseph, Simeon and Anna?

We might arrive with eagerness and leave with purpose, knowing that we can't keep to ourselves all we've seen and heard, because salvation has come, a light to the Gentiles, glory for God's people Israel, the redemption of Jerusalem and the world. All people — devout, depraved, righteous, sacrilegious, dutiful, derelict — need this good news, whether they know it or not. The time has come for us to share it.

## Lectionary Reflections

This week:

- Why do you go to worship? What difference does fasting, praying, and following God's rules make for us? For others?
- What do you expect when you go to worship? What do you experience?
- Who are the Simeons and Annas you have known? How have they influenced you or your understanding of the faith?
- Simeon blesses Mary and Joseph and then speaks a haunting word to them. What does it mean to be blessed?
- This text is about faithful people's response to meeting Jesus. Both Simeon and Anna praise God. How are we praising God in response to Jesus' birth?
- If you are making New Year's resolutions, how do they relate to your faith?

## Second Sunday After Christmas
Jeremiah 31:7-14; Ephesians 1:3-14; John 1: (1-9), 10-18

Adjectives abound this second Sunday after Christmas. The gospel lesson exudes descriptors of the Logos, of the Word made flesh, through whom all things came to being. This Word is life and light. This word has power to make us children of God. This Word is flesh and this flesh is known by its grace and truth, grace upon grace. The beauty of this passage from John soars with divine mystery and majesty because human words cannot contain the glory of the most high God.

Ephesians provides an antiphonal response to the first chapter of John's gospel, revealing the impact of all of those divine characteristics. Through the Word, through Jesus Christ, we mortals are blessed and chosen, adopted and redeemed, gathered and made heirs of God and marked with the seal of the Holy Spirit.

Prose feels inadequate as poetry marks the biblical texts for this week. Jeremiah provides a clue as to how we ought to respond to such glory and grace, truth and redemption. Those scattered are now gathered from the farthest parts of the earth, those radiant with the goodness of the Lord, can only erupt in praise, sing and rejoice. Might that be a word for us this week?

As we reflect on the incarnation and move forward into a new calendar year, could we preachers and teachers of the faith call for a season of unabashed praise for all that God has done, all that God is doing, and all that God will do? More than gratitude praise incorporates our entire being, praise reflects back into the world the radiant goodness of our God, praise refuses to be embarrassed by evident emotions of joy made known in shouts or tears, dance or song, poetry or prose. Such demonstrative shows of delight, wonder and joy would garner the attention of others given, their rarity. Outrage we see. Righteous indignation we know well. Cynicism is all too familiar. Boredom typical. Numbness and skepticism the stock and trade of our culture. But when was the last time you witnessed or experienced or participated in unmitigated praise in the face of God's glorious beauty and truth, light and power, grace and goodness?

What might it look like for us to show our redemption or blessedness, that we are marked with the seal of the Holy Spirit? Imagine if the goodness of our God radiated from the walls of our sanctuaries and out into God's beloved world. Sometimes I think that Jesus' admonishment that we must be like children if we are to enter the kingdom of heaven has something to do with the unfiltered nature of children. When they hurt, they cry. When they are frustrated, they scream. When they are delighted, they squeal. When they are happy, they laugh. They radiate that which is within them at any given moment. As we grow older, we learn to mask our feelings, emotions, hopes, vulnerabilities. This is, of course, often appropriate and healthy. However, this greater control sometimes stunts our very being and prevents us from fully living the life God gives. We stop seeing the wonder in all creation. We miss the light-filled, grace-filled, truth-filled word still speaking all around us. We worry about what others might think if we exhibit too much joy, lament, praise, or angst. Now is the time to live as the children of God Jesus empowers us to be.

Many afternoons when I am sitting in my car outside my daughters' high school, waiting for the final bell of the day to ring, I am gifted with an enfleshed, grace-filled, illuminating word. The children in the special education classes get dismissed a few minutes early, their teachers walking them to their respective buses. Almost without fail, they radiate a sense of joy as they make their way out of the building. They skip. They hold their teachers' hands. They stop to hug a fellow classmate or pause to look at something they find interesting. The teachers appear to be happy, too. They do not rush. They stop and observe with their students. They receive and give hugs. I observe and find myself both delighted and reminded to notice the grace, the glory, the life, the light, the community, the children, right in front of me. In those moments I remember to praise God for the gift of being alive and gathered, chosen and blessed.

The texts appointed for this second Sunday after Christmas invite us to silence that voice within us that tells us to keep everything under control, do not expect too much, do not hope too much, do not reveal too much, to not rejoice or grieve too much, and instead give ourselves over to the Word made flesh and embodied in us. Allow the Word to overwhelm and envelop, silence in you any voice but God's. Open your mouth, your body, your whole Jesus-redeemed being to praise and song, truth, grace upon grace, let it radiate through you so that you will be, we will be, the light of the world no darkness can overcome.

This week:

- Read the text from John and then the one appointed from Ephesians. Do you see the connections? What words are present in both texts?

- When was the last time you experienced pure praise? When were you lost in wonder? Joy? Song?

- What does it mean to you that you are a child of God? What does it mean to you that others are children of God?

- Read the adjectives that describe the Word made flesh. Pick one to focus on each day of this week. At the end of the day, write down where you saw that characteristic of Jesus present in the world.

- Read the adjectives that describe the impact of Jesus Christ for human beings. Make these words the focus of your prayers this week and notice how this focus shapes your decisions, interactions and words.

- Have you ever felt scattered? Have you ever been displaced? Far away from home? What was it like? How did it feel to be gathered from those places?

## Baptism of the Lord/Epiphany 1/Ordinary Time 1
Genesis 1:1-5; Acts 19:1-7; Mark 1:4-11

In the very beginning of a new year, we remember Jesus' baptism.

Mark, as usual, was into that whole brevity thing — leaving out any hesitancy on John's part to baptize the one who came after him, but who is above him. Jesus didn't explain the reason for his baptism, either. In Mark we simply get a recounting of the events: Jesus was baptized by John in the Jordan. Jesus saw the heavens torn apart and the Spirit descending like a dove on him. (Did anyone else see these spectacular happenings? Did John? Mark didn't say.) God spoke from heaven, proclaiming that Jesus was God's beloved Son with whom God was well pleased. Even without questions, commentary, or explanation, the account resonates with miraculous meaning.

Ordinary water employed by very human John became the catalyst for heaven rending, Spirit descending, God announcing, identity giving action. No ordinary day at the Jordan for John, or for Jesus. And yet, how often do we consider that Jesus' baptism resounds in our own and in that of our brothers and sisters in Christ? Few pastors lack stories of parents requesting to have the baby "done" or "christened." Many a congregation has giggled when the baby cried as the minister struggled to get through the liturgy. Most of us have been moved when a parent of an infant or an adult being baptized has renounced evil and professed their faith. But do we consider that in our baptism the barrier between heaven and earth has been torn asunder, the Spirit has alighted on our head and God has claimed us and called us beloved?

I wonder if we are not more like those new converts that Paul questions in Acts who responded to his query about their baptism with an honest, "We have not even heard that there is a Holy Spirit." We have not even thought about the impact of our baptism. We have not claimed the promise or shuttered at the responsibility. We have not recognized the new day, the beginning, ushered in by the baptism of Jesus and our own baptism. It is the first day of the rest of our new lives in Christ and nothing will ever be the same again.

The study catechism, approved for use in 1998 at the 210th General Assembly of the Presbyterian Church (U.S.A.), says this:

*Question 71: What is baptism?*

*Answer: Baptism is the sign and seal through which we are joined to Christ.*

*Question 72: What does it mean to be baptized?*

*Answer: My baptism means that I am joined to Jesus Christ forever. I am baptized into his death and resurrection, along with all who have received him by faith. As I am baptized with water, he baptizes me with his Spirit, washing away all my sins and freeing me from their control. My baptism is a sign that one day I will rise with him in glory and may walk with him even now in newness of life.*

The day you were baptized, or had your children baptized, or baptized a new member of the Body of Christ, was no ordinary day in the sanctuary. No ordinary day in the Jordan for John, for Jesus, or for us because Jesus' baptism demonstrated the lengths to which God will go to be reconciled with us and to reconcile us to one another. God tore apart the heavens to get to us, to give us the Holy Spirit, to forgive us and join us to Christ. Do we recognize into what, into whom, we were baptized?

At the start of a new calendar year, reaffirming our baptism could remind us that the answer to that critical question is Jesus Christ. As we make resolutions or renew commitments to get in shape, get out of debt, or check a few items off our bucket list, as Christians we should also turn away from the ways of sin and renounce evil and its power in the world. We should publicly turn to Jesus Christ and accept him as our Lord and Savior, trusting in his grace and love. We should reaffirm again that we will be Christ's faithful disciples, obeying his word and showing his love. In other words, we should make sure that our baptism marked the first day of the rest of our lives as beloved children of God, anointed us with the Holy Spirit, and empowered to do God's will.

As I reflect on this baptism of the Lord Sunday, I think about pivotal moments in my faith journey. One of which took place just a few years ago. I remember and I struggle with the contrast I experienced on August 12, 2017, in Charlottesville, Virginia. The hope I felt gathered for worship at sunrise in a Baptist sanctuary packed with people of every color, multiple faiths and no faith at all, tethers me to the vision of John in Revelation of every tribe and nation worshiping God together; their differences still visible, but their unity of praise and purpose unstoppable. And yet, the vitriolic, calculated, organized hate I saw that day and the night before and in the days since won't leave me alone. And it shouldn't. It had better not, frankly. I continue to be compelled to announce both ends of the humanity I witnessed: the light and the dark, the good and the evil, the hope and the horror. Healing won't happen without an honest account of both.

Many days I still wonder what will happen next and what role I am to play in this story that started long before my baptism and will continue, I am sure, long after my baptism is complete in my death. I keep praying for wisdom, discernment, and a means to make an impact for good. Too often I feel utterly useless, a noisy gong and a clanging cymbal in a world already awash in a distracting din of rhetoric. And yet, I can't turn and leave or throw up my hands in despair because I am baptized. By virtue of my baptism, I am united to Christ and through Christ to you and, because of Christ, to the whole of creation. And I can't undo that unity, no matter how hard I try. We are stuck together. In baptism we are clothed in Christ, made one with Christ, the Body of Christ, the church, and our neighbors — the body of humanity made in God's image and called good. And while this is transformative for us, it is not for our sake only; it is for the sake of God's beloved creation.

This Sunday, I am going to remember that Jesus was baptized and that heaven was subsequently torn apart and the Holy Spirit escaped and the Son of God — the one who pleases God, the one God so loves, and who so loves the world — frees me from my sins and their control so that I can right now walk in newness of life. Today, therefore, is a new day, the first day of the rest of my life, a day to renounce evil, turn to

Jesus Christ, obey his word, show his love and trust the Holy Spirit to do the rest.

This week:

- If you are baptized, what do you know about your baptism? How often do you remember your baptism? What difference does it make to you that you are baptized?
- John Calvin wrote, "But if it was the baptism of God, it surely had enclosed in itself, the promise of forgiveness of sins, the mortification of the flesh, spiritual vivification, and participation in Christ." Can you put into contemporary language each of those four meanings of baptism?
- Where are other places in scripture where the heavens are opened? (For examples, see Ezekiel 1:1; John 1:51; Acts 10:11; and Revelation 19:11.) Any commonalities?
- Have you ever participated in or witnessed a memorable baptism? What was memorable about it and why?
- Look up "baptism" in the index of the Presbyterian Church (U.S.A.)'s Book of Confessions and compare what various confessions have to say about baptism. What meanings and images do you see repeated? Which ones resonate (or not) with you?
- Daily pray to remember your baptism and ask God to help you make it visible in the world.

## Epiphany 2/Ordinary Time 2
1 Samuel 3:1-19 (11-20); 1 Corinthians 6:12-20; John 1:43-51

"See for yourself," Philip told a skeptical Nathanael.

Philip cannot contain his excitement over meeting Jesus, recognizing early on that Jesus, son of Joseph from Nazareth, is the one about whom Moses in the law and also the prophets spoke about. Nathanael's assumptions rendered him unable to imagine the possibility, "Can anything good come out of Nazareth?" Imagine the equivalent of Nathanael's quip in contemporary culture. For some it might be, "Can anything good come out of Washington, DC?" For others it might be bias against religion or particular forms of religion that could be a stumbling block to recognizing the divine. "Can anything good come out of _____?" Fill in the blank based on your own context. In some communities, it will be neighborhoods that come to mind. For others, it will be certain professions. In some places there are entire categories of people deemed godforsaken, written off as "trailer trash," "thugs," or the like.

For Nathanael, Nazareth was a small, backwater town (or "backhoe town" as one of my children used to say), no place for God's chosen to call home. Philip didn't argue. In our day of constant debate accompanied by the relentless need to be right, Philip's response was worth noting. Philip didn't defend Nazareth saying: "Have you ever even been to Nazareth? It is beautiful this time of year. Lots of lovely people in Nazareth." Nor did he chide Nathanael for his biases or call him out for his lack of cultural sensitivity. He simply said, "Come and see." Don't believe me? Come see for yourself.

Philip issued an invitation, not unlike Jesus' invitation to Philip a few verses back, "Follow me." In the earlier part of the story prior to the appointed verses for this Sunday, to those disciples of John who are curious about where Jesus is staying he said, "Come and see." No sales pitch. No promises of what they will discover. No cajoling or guilt or reward or expectations. Just an invitation, no strings attached. How often do we receive or extend such genuine invitations?

We receive invitations to events that are really a summons. There will be a price to pay for not showing up. (Some family gatherings fit this category. The office holiday party in some places does too.) We receive invitations that come with the expectation that we bring something to the event: food, a friend, our best behavior. We get invitations where we are sure to be asked to give something once we get there: money, advice, praise. There are even those invitations to "parties" that are really occasions where we will be sold something: clothing, skincare, a time-share.

How often do we simply say or hear "come and see"? You may accept or decline. You may come exactly as you are. No need to get changed, bring a hostess gift, or even RSVP. Your cynicism, skepticism, biases, assumptions are all welcome as well. You can stay as long as you like or leave without notice. Maybe everything you have ever heard and believed about Nazareth will be confirmed. No one will attempt to convince you otherwise. Come and see.

What might happen if we church people emulated Jesus and Philip in this story and stopped being defensive and started being invitational instead? What if we were honestly open to whatever opinion others may have about us, about Jesus, about the church, about Christians? Nothing good can come out of Christianity. "Come and see." Christians are judgmental and exclusive. "Come and see." All they do in church is ask for money. "Come and see." Worship is boring. "Come and see." The institution of the church is irrelevant. "Come and see." No one will speak to me. "Come and see." People will judge me for how I look or talk or think or believe. "Come and see." I am beyond redemption. "Come and see." No one ever really changes. "Come and see."

Like Philip, we are not to cajole, convince, sell, or sugarcoat. We are to share our experience of following Jesus Christ and invite others to come and see Jesus for themselves. How often do we unabashedly tell others about Jesus and his impact on us and then invite them to get to know him, too? No guilt. No empty promises. No expectation that their experience will be identical to our own. No need for them to confirm our choices or beliefs. No requirement that they agree with us. No defensiveness or debating. Just: Come and see Jesus for yourself.

There are some things in this world that I so love, I want others to love them too: the Bible, the church, worship, Jesus. (Maybe not in that order.) Other things, like books, the smell of chlorine mixed with the humid air of an indoor swimming pool in the wee hours of the morning, my pets, my children, my quirky family, (maybe not in that order) coffee, red wine, butterscotch ice cream and green beans cooked with fatback (probably in that order). Yet everything I list can only be experienced to be appreciated (or not). I can describe their qualities, wax elegantly about why I value them, defend them until I am blue in the face — but if anyone has any chance of loving the church, my children, coffee, and, yes, Jesus, they first must come and experience for themselves what I have come to know and love. Even then, I can't control their experiences or evaluations or responses to any of the above, from worship to my aggressively loving golden retriever.

What I can control is whether or not I honestly invite others to experience those things, people, and places I can't imagine my life without and that begins with Jesus and his body, the church.

I confess that my greatest challenge to following Philip's example comes within my own household. I desperately want my children to follow Jesus and be a part of a community of faith. Some of my reasons for that desire are completely selfish, I realize. I want them to have the support, encouragement, and network of people that comes with that connection. Knowing they have such a community will relieve me of some stress as they move through life's various stages. (It is all about me.) However, I also believe that they will have life and have it abundantly, regardless of their circumstances, if they accept Jesus' invitation to come and follow him. But I can't make them, or anyone for that matter, accept Jesus' call. I can't convince them of the truth of the gospel or the goodness of God. I can, however, haltingly attempt to live that truth and goodness so that they might glimpse enough of it to be open to my invitation to them to come and see Jesus for themselves, despite all their assumptions about Nazareth.

This week:

- What are some of your assumptions that might prevent you from being open to God's presence? Are there people and places that you have a difficult time imagining God working in or through? Why?

- When is the last time you invited someone to come and see Jesus? How did it go? What keeps you from doing so?

- What are the assumptions you run up against when you are open about your faith or beliefs? How do you respond to those assumptions when they are voiced?

- In the reading for this Sunday from 1 Samuel, Samuel needs Eli's help discerning God's voice. Who has helped you hear God's instructions? How have you helped others discern God's call?

- How do you follow Jesus daily? Do you think about following Jesus throughout the day? As you make decisions or interact with others?

- Take a look at other passages where Philip is mentioned in John's gospel (John 6:5, 7, John 12:21, John 14:8). What characteristics do you notice about Philip? Can you relate to him in your own faith journey?

## Epiphany 3/Ordinary Time 3
Jonah 3:1-5, 10; 1 Corinthians 7:29-31; Mark 1:14-20

God told Jonah to go to Nineveh and proclaim God's message. Check.

The people of Nineveh heard the message and responded with repentance and a fast. Check. God, in turn, reversed course and did not bring upon them the proclaimed calamity. Check. No conflict. No questions. No complaining, negotiating, or bargaining. This selection from Jonah would make for a boring movie or novel. Everything is so neat and buttoned up. Everyone does what is right and good. Just like in your experience, right?

Then the gospel lesson for this week: Jesus went to Galilee. Check. He proclaimed the good news of God. Check. He told Simon and Andrew to follow him and they did. Check. Check. Same went for Zebedee's sons, James and John. Check. Check. No conflict. No questions. No complaining, negotiating, or bargaining. Again, not much of a plot here. Flat characters. Boring. Everything was so neat and buttoned up. Everyone did what is right and good. Just like in your experience, right?

These stories of call in Jonah and Mark follow a typical pattern, in some ways. But in other ways, they do not. We don't get Jeremiah's pushback about being too young or Moses' claim he doesn't talk well. No one in these pericopes worried about being unworthy or ill equipped. God called, they went. Is the point of these two lectionary readings to make us feel like lesser disciples? Is the point akin to the one made by our parents when they asked us why we couldn't be more like our brother, sister, or cousin? *Your brother never did that when he was your age. Your baby cousin can manage to sit through church.* Simon and Andrew left their nets immediately and followed. What? *You can't even give up chocolate for Lent? You can't manage to set aside an hour for worship each week? Tithe?* James and John left their father behind in the boat, for God's sake. Really!

But what about the *rest* of the story as Paul Harvey used to say. Take note of that caveat in Jonah 3:1. The Word of the Lord came to Jonah a *second* time.

And let's not forget what happened after Jonah's aquatic adventure and *after* his prophecy to Nineveh. He got mad that God dialed back the divine wrath. I wonder if Jonah thought that given God's character of mercy and steadfast love, God was going to relent regardless of his shouting and regardless of the people's repentance. Jonah seemed to say: "Why in the world did you put me through this, God? If you are going to make me cry out judgment, at least follow through with it!"

Then there is the rest of the story of the disciples in Mark. Keep in mind, we are only in chapter one and these fisherfolk have just started their Jesus journey. Jesus asked them why they had such little faith. Those eager followers sought to send away the hungry and children alike. Peter got that harsh rebuke from Jesus, "Get behind me Satan!" James and John, the very ones who dropped their nets like hot potatoes, requested a reward for their efforts, wanting to sit at Jesus' left and right. Peter, James, and John, three of the four of chapter one, fell asleep when Jesus, deeply agitated and in need of them, asked them to keep awake. Oh, and Peter denied Jesus thrice. Everyone did what was right and good? Not so much. Just like in your experience, right?

Perhaps the point of this call narrative is not so much to show us how much we pale in comparison to the spiritual greats of the Bible, but to help us understand that even our fervent faithfulness will falter and God uses us anyway. The rest of the story is an important part of these stories.

Jonah did what God told him to do. Eventually. Simon and Andrew, James and John, eagerly dropped everything and followed Jesus. Sometimes. Discipleship is a one step forward, two step back sort of endeavor. The inspiration we can derive from an obedient Jonah and wildly, inexplicably responsive fishermen is one of hope knowing that our dutifulness and fervor, even if intermittent, is useful and allows God to work even if such demonstrations of piety or prophecy aren't consistent.

We, too, will get angry at God and hope those Ninevites get their comeuppance. (It will feel so good to say "I told you so!") We, too, will want some divine compensation when we feel as if we sacrificed something on God's behalf. We, too, will send away the hungry, dismiss the vulnerable, fall asleep when staying awake is critical, and deny Jesus three times (or more). And yet, mad as Jonah may be about it, God is gracious and merciful, slow to anger and abounding in steadfast love, and ready to relent from punishing. We may bemoan that godly character when it spares those we wish would get what they had coming, but we sure do celebrate it when extended to us.

We can look to Jonah, post-big-fish, pre-wishing-to-die, and we can admire the immediate and total come-to-Jesus moment of Simon and Andrew, James, and John, but we should not imagine that their story of faith is all that different from our own. Obedience and recalcitrance, praise and complaint, faithfulness and apostasy, service and selfishness, awake and asleep, hospitable and withholding, saint and sinner, and human, yet called beloved by God.

No one does what is right and good all the time. Rarely are things neat and buttoned up. Often there are questions. Usually there is conflict. Almost always there is complaining, negotiating, bargaining. Isn't this your experience? It certainly is mine. And yet, because God is gracious and merciful, slow to anger and abounding in steadfast love, ready to relent from punishing, we can be bold to drop our nets and follow — imperfectly. Sometimes. Trusting that when we can't or don't or won't, God won't abandon us but instead will meet us where we are, give us some shade for a time, patiently teach us and, in the end, forgive and redeem us.

This week:

- Have you had seasons of eager discipleship when you dropped your nets and followed? What about times when you fell asleep when Jesus needed you most?
- How do you think Zebedee felt about James and John taking off and leaving him behind with the family business? Are there times that faithfulness to Jesus puts us at odds with responsibilities to family and friends?

- What are some skills that fishermen and fisherwomen have that might be useful to Christian discipleship?
- Take a look at other biblical passages that mention fish, fishing, or nets. For example: Jeremiah 16:16, Ezekiel 47:10, and Matthew 13:47. Notice any consistent themes? Marked differences?
- Could it be that Simon, Andrew, James, and John were happy to leave their work and follow Jesus? Are there days you wish Jesus would say: "Leave everything and follow me?"
- If you aren't called to drop everything and follow Jesus, what smaller things might you be called to drop or stop in order to follow Jesus more closely or better?

## Epiphany 4/Ordinary Time 4
Deuteronomy 18:15-20; I Corinthians 8:1-13; Mark 1:21-28

What an exciting day at the synagogue. Astounding teaching, interrupted by an angry outburst, followed by a convulsion filled exorcism.

No one in attendance would ever forget this week's worship. No wonder Jesus' fame began to spread throughout the surrounding region of Galilee. Who wouldn't have been talking about such an experience?

In eight short verses, Mark covered a lot of ground. The gospel emphasized the distinctiveness of Jesus' teaching as one with authority — not like the scribes, who presumably interpreted or quoted the work of other rabbis and scholars. Jesus, on the other hand, spoke for himself (and of himself, although they don't know this yet). The issue of Jesus' authority comes up frequently in Mark's gospel. All creation is under Jesus' authority: waves and wind, demons and diseases. Jesus' astounding teaching was coupled with Jesus' astonishing deeds, a truth evident at the very beginning of his ministry. Jesus, whoever he is, was not like the other religious leaders of the day. He brought a new teaching and even the unclean spirits obey him.

Imagining the reaction of those gathered that sabbath is a stretch given our familiarity with all that comes after this early story in Mark. We know who Jesus is: the Messiah, the Son of God. We know his authority is divine. We know he is Lord of all. We know he is the risen and victorious one who sits on the right hand of God judging the quick and the dead. The people who came to synagogue that sabbath knew none of this, at least not then. How, then, can we fathom the experience of witnessing Jesus teaching and healing apart from all that came after those first days of his ministry?

No wonder everyone kept asking in amazement, "What is this?"

I wonder if, even with all we know about Jesus, we might benefit from asking the same question in our contexts.

What is this new teaching?

What power are we witnessing?

What are the demons Jesus casts out?

What do we do now that we have witnessed this extraordinary experience?

If we aren't pondering these questions, then maybe we need to head to synagogue and hear Jesus' teachings again. If we aren't astounded and amazed by what Jesus is doing in the world, then we aren't paying attention. In the words of Deuteronomy, we are not heeding the word of God's prophet.

Mark's gospel presented Jesus as coming to confront and vanquish evil. When the man with the unclean spirit burst on the scene and asked, "Have you come to destroy us?" the answer was a resounding, "Yes!" Jesus had come to destroy evil and save the world possessed by it. The "just then" of this text marks an important transition where Jesus' teaching was put into transformative action. Jesus did not talk about the saving work of God, he enacted it. Jesus' new, authoritative teaching crushed the powers of darkness and set people free to be their God-created selves. The demons were the first to recognize Jesus' identity and power because they were the very ones he came to destroy. All the more reason for us to be on the lookout for the convulsing of evil spirits as a sure sign that the Holy One of God is nearby and we should draw closer to him.

I recognize that talk of evil, demons, and unclean spirits does not resound with familiarity in our day and time. In fact, I admit, it sounds a little nutty. However, reading the daily news renders it difficult to deny that darkness is pervasive and requires nothing less than God's intervention to bring light and wholeness. The challenge isn't to find the evil, rather it is to see the places where the formally possessed are clothed and in their right mind, and then to celebrate that wholeness, not disbelieve it, fear of it, or beg Jesus to leave our neighborhood because of it.

That's an odd reality of Jesus' healings and exorcisms: Those who witness them often wish Jesus had left things, and people, as he found them. We are all too comfortable with the status quo, even when it is demonic and devastating to some.

This week's gospel lesson is about Jesus, not about us, though. Our role in this story is limited. Those who witnessed Jesus' astounding teaching and power showed up to worship and then talked about what they experienced. They asked one another what it might mean and then they told others who had not seen for themselves about this extraordinary teacher. They spoke the truth about what had transpired, proclaiming that even the unclean spirits obeyed him. Surely, they were not the same after such an encounter with the Holy One of God, even if they could not fully understand or explain what happened. Is not the same true for us?

I have never once witnessed a dramatic exorcism in worship (or anywhere). I have, however, seen dramatic transformations, healing and light inexplicably overcoming darkness. Often these inbreakings of good have occurred over time, not shazam-like on a Sunday morning. Nonetheless, they are worthy of amazement and sharing.

I have known beloved children of God racked with addiction, now sober and reaching out to others trying to get clean. I have known families sleeping in their cars, now living in homes of their own through their own hard work and the help of those willing to walk alongside them. I have known couples estranged and bitter, now reconnected, forgiving and forgiven, more committed to one another than ever before. I have known some who have exploited and cheated others, now repentant and working to make amends. In short, I have seen Jesus destroy all that threatens to possess and devastate God's beloved, for whom he wants abundant life. Often, I have been amazed. Sometimes I have been disbelieving. And, yes, there have been times I have wished Jesus had left things and people as they were because I didn't want to see my culpability in their suffering or because I didn't want to change my own behavior or because I in some way benefited from their painful circumstances.

Jesus took on and vanquished evil anyway. He was not like the scribes. His authority required no outside permission or affirmation. This story is all about Jesus. Our role is to bear witness to what we have seen, heard and experienced, to wrestle with what it is that Jesus was doing and, hopefully, celebrate and even participate in it. When we show up to the synagogue this sabbath and listen to Jesus, we should also be amazed and ask: What is this new teaching, and how can I follow it?

This week:

- Notice the "just then" in this story. Are there other stories in scripture that have a similar transition? What happens after "just then"? Have there been some "just then" moments you have experienced in worship or in other settings?
- Why is it that the demons were the ones who recognized Jesus' identity? Look at other passages where demons talk to Jesus (Mark 5:1-13, for example). What happened in those exchanges? How did the people around them react?
- Note other instances where people were astounded by Jesus' teaching. What were they astounded about? How did they respond to his teaching? (Mark 6:1-6; Mark 7:31-37; Mark 10:23-27; Mark 11:15-19)
- When have you witnessed an amazing transformation or turn around? What was it? How did it happen? How did you and others respond to it?
- Have you ever experienced a worship service that was amazing or astounding? If so, what about it made it so?
- Are you comfortable talking about demons, unclean spirits and/or evil? If not, why not? If so, why?

## Epiphany 5/Ordinary Time 5
Isaiah 40:21-31; 1 Corinthians 9:16-23; Mark 1:29-39

The reading for this morning depict four scenes and two settings.

The two settings? Simon's home and a deserted place. The four scenes? Healing of Simon's mother-in-law, scene one. The whole city clamoring at the door, scene two. Jesus praying alone, scene three. Jesus' prayer time interrupted by Simon and his companion who had come to let Jesus know everyone wanted him, scene four. If I were to make a film of this week's gospel lesson, I could choose several different directions. I could go with an emphasis on scene one and call it, "Healed to Serve" or maybe a more Lifetime network-esque, "Lifted Up by the Hand of Jesus." I could also go more with scene two and title it, "Banging at the Door for Healing" or "Sundown Miracles," or even "Silenced Demons." Scene three would make for a more indie-type film, lots of close ups of Jesus' face combined with broad views of desolate land. Let's call this story "No River Runs Through It" or "Dark and Deserted." Finally, scene four, "Hunted While Praying" or "Everyone is Searching for You" or "Mission Possible."

The influence of the Hollywood awards season aside, the back and forth between intimate and public, solitude and chaos, private time and corporate need, makes for dramatic tension in these verses. Jesus seemed to seek seclusion and prayer, only to be chased and hunted by those desperate for his healing power. He silenced the demons because they know who he was; regardless, the crowds kept coming having heard of his power. Nothing would quiet the fervor of those once sick and suffering now made whole. Once Jesus began to fulfill his mission, there was no turning back the tidal wave of humanity longing for the presence of God.

The tie that binds those two settings and four scenes together is the mission, Jesus' mission, to proclaim the message and cast out demons and bring healing. Suffering existed in Simon's household and throughout the surrounding neighborhoods. Deserted places and crowded cities yearned to hear God's good news. Preaching and healing could not be extricated from prayer. Jesus' mission kept him ever moving, leaving those who longed to have him stay, sending him to those who wished him dead. Jesus' message compelled him to find a refuge for prayer and motivated him to get up and go to Galilee. No matter the setting, no matter the scene, Jesus would do what he came to earth to do: proclaim the message, cast out demons, ease suffering, and defeat sin as disciples then and now scramble to pay attention and keep up.

Mark's gospel has a breathlessness to it — one scene quickly fades into another and the next. The reader, the disciple, must keep alert and watching because if we succumb to any distraction, we might lose Jesus and have to go hunting for him. Like Simon and his companion, we wake up and discover Jesus isn't where we left him or where we thought he'd be, and we must go out into the darkness to find him. Seems like a pretty good metaphor for faith, doesn't it? We need Jesus. There are countless others who need Jesus, too, some of them are asking us where he is, and we have no idea. Suffering abounds, the needs are overwhelming, and Jesus is not in the house. Jesus refuses to stay put. We cannot contain him. He is on a mission. A mission from God, no less, and all we can do is find him and follow.

We must look in deserted places of prayer and tumultuous places filled with demons and disease. We might find him in our house, tending to our mother-in-law or in the streets of neighborhoods where we've never been or wanted to go. If we are to find Jesus and follow him, we must share his mission because he will always be found where the message is proclaimed, demons are cast out, and wholeness is nurtured. Where there is gospel preaching, godly teaching and life-affirming healing happening, Jesus will be found, even if it isn't where we thought he would be.

I have heard the gospel preached and found Jesus present in strange places and unexpected people. I have been taught Jesus' new commandment to love one another through strangers. I have seen healing fight its way through deep wounds, leaving visible scars coupled with great joy. When crowds were banging on the door and looking for things

I did not have to give, amazingly Jesus appeared and did more than I could ever hope for or imagine. A multitude of settings, a myriad of changing scenes, deserted places, and noisy spaces, with Jesus fulfilling his mission in them all. I only had to keep hunting for him and follow. At times, I have had to strain in the darkness to see him, but eventually the dawn broke and he was there.

The news has been filled with brutality, cruelty, and violence. The serial sexual abuse of young, female gymnasts, the torture of thirteen children by their own parents, school shootings that have left students dead and lives shattered. The crowds are clamoring at the door, crying out for healing and help. Where is Jesus? Does he have the power to cast out these demons? Bring wholeness to this depth of brokenness? Is there a word of good news to be proclaimed to these communities? To ours?

I have been searching for Jesus, looking for gospel mercy, foot-washing love, and demon-crushing grace. The before-dawn darkness has made finding our servant Lord difficult, but I see glimpses of our Savior, whispers of his message and hints of his transformative mission at work. I read that thousands (thousands!) of people have called to offer help and support for the thirteen Turpin children. The local chamber of commerce put together a list of items needed, and the response was overwhelming. They have asked people to stop bringing things and said to please send money instead. So far, $50,000 has been raised. Seeing the list of shoe sizes, clothing needs, and the request for art supplies and hygiene items made those children's suffering gut-wrenchingly tangible. But seeing each item crossed off and noticing that every request had been fulfilled gave me hope that Jesus' mission, his message, his healing, and his casting out of demons would not be thwarted, no matter how deep the darkness or how powerful the demons.

There are some scenes in our current setting filled with suffering, sickness, and evil spirits; some present in the house next door, others played out in the streets, some private hells, and some public tragedies. And if we want to find Jesus, we need to pray and join him on his mission of preaching, teaching, and healing, until every member of the crowd, every member of every household, is made whole and well.

This week:

- Jesus healed Simon's mother-in-law and she got up to serve. How has Jesus healed you for you to serve him?
- When have you had to search for Jesus? Where and how did you find him?
- Jesus' mission required him to leave those who wanted him to stay. He was always on the move in Mark's gospel. How do we discern when to stay and when to move? When to keep serving in ways we currently serve and when to make a change?
- How do you balance prayer and contemplation with service and action? How are prayer and service connected?
- Imagine each scene in your mind's eye. What do you notice? Who are you? What is God's Word to you in this passage?
- Pray the headlines this week. Pull up a news website or look at the front page of your local paper. Pray for the people and places you read about there.

## Transfiguration of the Lord
2 Kings 2:1-12; 2 Corinthians 4:3-6; Mark 9:2-9

Calvin and Hobbes cartoon strips come to mind when I read the account of the Transfiguration of Jesus.

Do you remember Calvin's big cardboard box? He dubbed it a "transmogrifier," and told Hobbes the machine would turn you into something other than what you already are. Set the dial to the desired new thing and away you go into a bug or dinosaur or whatever you wrote on the side of the box. I equate Calvin's cardboard box with Peter's suggestion of building booths and Jesus' dazzling appearance with setting the dial to "Son of God." In an instant, Jesus appeared to be someone other than simply Joseph's boy from Nazareth. He looked markedly and substantively different. He had been transmogrified, and those on the mountain with him could not help but notice the change.

Much had happened prior to this mountain top experience. Demons had been cast out, lepers healed, parables told. A girl had even been brought back to life. Jesus walked on water, thousands had been fed, and Peter declared that Jesus was in fact the Messiah, all before Moses and Elijah appeared and God boomed a divine decree from the cloud. So, what's the big deal about the Transfiguration? What gets revealed in this story that wasn't already been revealed? What did Peter, James, and John know after this event that they didn't know before?

In short: They saw Jesus in a whole new light. All they knew and had witnessed, as miraculous and astounding as those things were, did not reveal the entirety of Jesus' identity. Peter's declaration that Jesus was the Messiah got prophetic, historic, and transcendent confirmation through the Transfiguration. Jesus indeed is the Messiah, the one of whom the prophets spoke, the one who fulfills the law, the one who is from God and of God and to whom they should listen. It is noteworthy the Transfiguration is bracketed in Mark's gospel by Jesus predicting his passion. Jesus, dazzlingly clothed, flanked by Elijah and Moses, heralded by God, would be the one who would be betrayed, killed, and who in three days would rise from the dead, his appearance different yet again, but his identity the same. Jesus was not, after all, transmogrified, turned from one thing into another. Jesus of Nazareth is the beloved Son of God, the Messiah, fully human, fully divine, executed, buried, raised, and ascended. He will not be contained by booth, nor by grave. No wonder the disciples were at a loss for words.

Peter, James, and John saw Jesus in a whole new light, one so bright, so otherworldly, that they were left terrified and tongue-tied. Jesus, the one who healed the sick and walked on water, the Messiah, the Son of God, the fulfillment of law and prophets, the one to whom they should listen and follow. Perhaps the greatest transformation that took place on the mountain was not Jesus' Transfiguration, but the disciples' understanding of the magnitude and majesty of their Savior. In seeing Jesus in a whole new light, there was hope that they would begin to see themselves and this mission in a whole new light, too, beginning with the hard truth that the Messiah did not allow his disciples to stay in safe spaces far above the chaos and needs of the world.

When have we been so overwhelmed with Jesus' majesty and magnitude that our proximity to him has left us stuttering, awed, and unsure of what to do next? When have we thought we knew everything there was to know about our Lord, only to be ambushed by the realization that we know nothing about him at all? Maybe it has been a mountaintop experience, accompanied by visions and a voice from heaven. Maybe it has been in the words of a fellow disciple or the off-handed remarks of a stranger, or the strains of a familiar hymn or the recitation of poem, prayer, or creed. In short: When have we seen Jesus in a whole new light, and as a result seen ourselves and God's mission in a whole new light too?

My discipleship has transmogrified — escaped the booth or box in which I had placed it — time and time again through the influence and example of those who follow Jesus more closely and better than I. I have come to see Jesus and subsequently his mission, others, and myself, in a new light altogether when people who have been egregiously wronged have offered forgiveness, and those who've wounded others have done everything they can think of to make amends. I have been left not knowing what to say when I have witnessed generosity extended without the slightest thought of reciprocity. I have wanted to preserve for the ages moments when I knew without question that God was speaking, only to realize that those moments live on only when they send us out into a world desperate to hear them.

Recently, I spent some time in a taxi in San Francisco. I made conversation with the driver. Originally from Iran, he had been in the United States many years, retiring from the trucking business only to realize that he couldn't live off of his social security payments. That's what got him driving a cab, sixteen hours a day, four days a week. It was the cost of housing, he said, "that kills you," that makes such unrelenting demands. "Sometimes," he said, "we really suffer." He lived an hour from the city because it was cheaper, but still making ends meet was still a challenge. Not long before we arrived at my destination, he asked what I did for a living. I told him I was a pastor. He asked if I preached every week. "Most weeks," I said. Our conversation drifted to the beauty of the place around us, the many things there were to do in the area, "if you have money."

He pulled over to the curb, I paid, and he got out to get my bag. As he handed my suitcase to me he said, "Pray for me." Then emphatically again, "Pray for me." I asked his name. I told him mine. Suddenly, I saw him in a whole new light. Not just a cab driver, but my brother, one for whom I had been entrusted to pray. I saw Jesus in a whole new light, too. Not the one I flew across the country to speak about. Not the one who was present on the seminary campus where I was to stay. Not one contained in the boxes in which I place him, but one who transcends any limits I try to impose upon him, more majestic than the mountains in the distance, and yet as close as the person right in front of me. In those moments of revelation and transfiguration, I don't know what to say, but I am left only to listen, for God, to Jesus, in the clouds and in taxis too.

This week:

- When has your understanding of Jesus changed? What caused your understanding to shift?

- Have you ever had a "mountaintop" experience that you wanted to preserve? What was different after that exceptional experience of the holy?
- Why is it important that Moses and Elijah were part of this story? How did they represent continuity with Jesus and God's salvation history?
- Where are other Bible passages where God's presence is revealed and concealed through a cloud? Look at Exodus 24:15 and Exodus 40:34, for examples. What's the significance of the cloud?
- Read the other accounts of the Transfiguration. What are the unique elements in each account? What do those distinct details reveal? (Matthew 17:1-9, and Luke 9:28-36)
- How do we listen to Jesus?

## Ash Wednesday
Isaiah 58:1-12; 2 Corinthians 5:20b-6:10; Matthew 6:1-6, 16-21


The publicly pious make a show of their righteousness and religion. The Christian show-off needs adoration, full credit, a photo op for serving at the soup kitchen or making a charitable donation. Their prayers and rituals, while done in the name of God, appear to be orchestrated to make themselves look good. The televangelist is almost a parody of this scenario, complete with bad behavior behind the scenes. We know the stories of those big falls from grace when the theme parks are left to deteriorate after the financial malfeasance, finally discovered, bringing down the showy, religious empire. All that fasting and praying, those on-camera sacrifices and service, none of it, really, was about or for God. No shortage of scandals has rocked the church since its beginning. Popes and priests, pastors and deacons, on large stages and in small, tucked away pulpits have been like those white-washed tombs Jesus talked about later in Matthew's gospel — brilliant on the outside but utterly corrupt just below the surface.

Finding and pointing to such fallenness in others, in whole institutions even, does not, however, invite us to examine our own complicity and daily lack of integrity. Ash Wednesday begins with us and then ripples out into our congregations and communities. Confession and repentance start with reflecting on our own motives, means, actions, and inactions. The gift of Lent entails accountability, honesty and, thanks to God, forgiveness and transformation. The gift of Lent that begins with Ash Wednesday every year is the opportunity God gives us to recognize where we have fallen short, so we can receive God's grace and mercy then turn to do and be better.

We live in a call-out culture, where publicly shaming others for their shortcomings big and small is prevalent. Social media allows everyone, everywhere, to point out the blind spots and hypocrisy of whomever they wish. Ash Wednesday is decidedly different than such mutual finger pointing. Ash Wednesday moves us away from scrutinizing the short-comings of others and calls us to the sometimes painful and life-long discipline of first examining our own failings.

Ash Wednesday calls us to consider when our calling out of others in the name of righteousness has really been about showing off our own superiority to others. Ash Wednesday invites us to look first and foremost at our own lack of integrity and address it with God, rather than demonstrating to the world just how good, righteous, and godly we are. All of these texts ask us to look inward in order to look outward, rightly first to God, and then in service to others.

Religious ritual without genuine care for the most vulnerable is an affront to God. Piety that does not increase the public good angers God, rather than pleases God. We are, after all, ambassadors for Christ, the one who came not to be served but to serve. God chooses to alleviate the burdens of the oppressed and to feed the hungry. If our means do not match God's ideals, we become a stumbling block and an obstacle to others; our witness is marred and our religion rightfully held in disdain.

Given the often earned bad reputation of institutional religion, Ash Wednesday allows individual disciples and corporate faith communities the opportunity to confess, repent, turn and attempt to live lives of service and integrity, in all circumstances, with patience, kindness, love, and truthful speech. Ash Wednesday litanies, the imposition of soot on our foreheads, the additional spiritual practices, the giving up of some treasured pleasure, or the taking on of acts of service, all mean nothing if they are not accompanied by compassionate, tangible, care for those less fortunate than ourselves, done not for show, but for the sake of the God who forgives and frees us. Our motives will never be pure. Inevitably, we will sin and fall short of the glory of God. We will do the very things we hate and we will fail to do the good we know. Nonetheless, God sent God's son to save us. There is grace. Mercy abounds. Ash Wednesday reminds us that God calls us out in order to call us up. God's judgment does not leave us ashamed and guilt ridden, but releases us to be more and more Christ-like as we seek to be honest with ourselves, transparent with the God who already knows everything about us, and ethical with others in everything in order to bear witness to the one who takes on our sin and that of all the world.

This week:

- Take time in private prayer to consider if your means match God's ends. When have you lived with integrity this past year? When have you fallen short?
- How does it feel to have someone put ashes on your forehead and tell you that, "you are dust, and to dust you will return?" Why is this reminder of our finitude important?
- When is it important to call out another's hypocrisy or sin? How do we go about this in ways that reflect the will and character of Jesus Christ?
- What spiritual practices help you focus on God and serve others?
- What spiritual practices will you take on this Lent?
- In what ways are you and your community of faith practicing a fast that is pleasing to God?

**First Sunday in Lent**

Genesis 9:8-17; 1 Peter 3:18-22; Mark 1:9-15

Mark's Holy Spirit dove does not sit cooing on a nearby branch, placidly watching.

No, Mark's version of the Holy Spirit was an angry bird, long before the video game came on the scene. The descending dove tore apart heaven to get to earthly Jesus as he came up out of the waters of baptism. The Holy Spirit drove out and forced Jesus to leave, expelled him, still dripping from the Jordan, into the wilderness to be tempted by Satan. Somehow that image of a gentle bird, branch in its mouth, doesn't do Mark's Holy Spirit justice. The turkey vultures circling above the unfortunate opossum torn asunder on my country road seem a more apt metaphor here. I'd hate to see what would have happened to Jesus if God had *not* been well pleased with him. Perhaps God's affirmation comes with a few strings to which one would rather not be attached.

So much is packed in so few verses: Jesus' baptism — heaven torn apart — the Holy Spirit breaking out from the heavenly confines and alighting on Jesus — the voice from heaven proclaiming Jesus' identity, status, and favor — a Spirit induced chase into the wilderness filled with wild beasts — Satan tempting Jesus for forty days — and angels waiting on Jesus for an unspecified duration. All this before Jesus began his ministry. I will take door number two, please. Give me the ministry prep of Hebrew, Greek, and ordination exams any day over wilderness, wild beasts, and Satan.

The question that begs asking is: Why? Why did Jesus' mission require such an arduous season of preparation? Did he glean special knowledge? Was this wilderness season akin to spiritual boot camp? Or an initiation process? A rite of passage? He had no Yoda, no master teacher, or mentor to guide him — only beasts and angels as he stood up against Satan. Unless, of course, the "angry bird" dove remained with him the whole time. I'd like to think that's the case. A heaven-busting, Messiah-expelling Holy Spirit is exactly the member of the Trinity I'd

65

like on my side in the wilderness with the wild beasts and Satan. There are times when a gentle cooing dove just doesn't cut it and surely this time of trial, temptation, and testing was one of those times.

Perhaps that's the lesson Jesus — beloved, Son of God, though he was — most needed to learn. Perhaps that's the lesson any one of we children of God need to know, not in theory, but through hard won experience. The power of the one who names us, claims us, calls us good, and sends us, remains with us always, tearing asunder the barriers between us and heaven, expelling us from safety, and upholding us through the wilderness, saving us from the wild beasts and sending angels along the way to nurture us while we wait for gentler seasons.

I am grateful for Mark's angry bird. I need to know that God's loving kindness comes coupled with unmistakable power; power to break down anything that keeps earth walled off from heaven, power that overpowers me and my desires, power that never turns back from truly scary places, like hospitals and prisons, battlefields and burial grounds, the deep recesses of my mind and the dark corners of my heart, power that doesn't turn back from beasts or evil, deserts or storms, power that summons angels to come where humans fear to tread. I don't think the Holy Spirit is so much like those turkey vultures but rather as blackbirds and chickadees, relentlessly chasing away any hawks that threaten to harm their young. That's the divine interference we need if we are going to survive the inhospitable, frightening, evil seasons that come when we are sent to do the work of God in the world that does not recognize the very one who came to save it.

Did Jesus remember those forty days as he went around Galilee preaching and healing, facing off with Pharisees, dealing with the rejection by the fine folks of his hometown, praying alone in the garden of Gethsemane, standing in front of Pilate and hanging on the cross? Those wilderness seasons marked by deprivation, loneliness, and beasts within and without strip us of all our illusions of control and self-sufficiency. They also reveal angels. We learn what (and who) sustains us, upholds us, and keeps all that would threaten to utterly destroy us at bay. We recognize the presence and power of the Holy Spirit, that angry bird who will stop at nothing to protect us and tear apart heaven to reach us.

Lent began on Ash Wednesday with ashes, prayers of confession, and declarations of penitence. While the Spirit may not have driven us into the wilderness, we are likely no strangers to times of deep fear and profound questioning. Lent reminds us that Jesus isn't either. Thanks be to God for that truth. There is no temptation, no beast, no demonic encounter left Godforsaken. The Holy Spirit, who took a nose-dive from the heavens to alight on the baptized does not retreat to a divine observation deck, but instead stays with us wherever we go, from wilderness to mountain top, heading off hawks and vultures and sending angels all along the way.

While we fast and pray, give up some things and take on others, Lent invites us to also mark the forty days that mark Jesus' forty days in the wilderness facing off Satan by remembering that our darkest seasons are not godforsaken, they are Spirit-infused. This in no way lessens the reality of the suffering, doubt, and even agony of wild beasts and seemingly inadequate angels. It does, however, remind us that we are not alone and proclaims that our state is not indicative of our status with God. We are God's beloved children, with whom God is well pleased, even when we find ourselves sorely tempted, afraid, and uncertain about our future. The angry bird circling above isn't out to get us, but instead relentlessly working to keep us safe until we get to Easter.

This week:

- How do you picture the Holy Spirit? There are various images in scripture: wind, dove, and flame. Do these images resonate with you? Why? Are there other images?
- What do you make of the almost violent words in this passage? Words like "expel" and "torn"? Are there other biblical stories that portray the Spirit as gentle? Is it important for the Holy Spirit to have both characteristics?
- How do you mark Lent? What Lenten practices do you find meaningful? Why?

- How does this story of Jesus' temptation relate to the petition in the Lord's Prayer, "Lead us not into temptation"? What are our temptations?

- Compare Mark's very short version of Jesus' temptation in the wilderness with the accounts in Luke and Matthew. Does it matter that Mark doesn't list the temptations? Is it useful to *not* have them listed?

- During challenging seasons in your life, what has sustained you? What did you learn about yourself? God? Others?

## Second Sunday in Lent
Genesis 17:1-7, 15-16; Romans 4:13-25; Mark 8:31-38

Immediately after Peter declared that Jesus was the Messiah, Jesus began to teach the disciples that he would "undergo great suffering."

He was rejected by the religious leaders of the day. He was killed. After three days, he rose again. Mark told us, "He said all this quite openly." A stark contrast to His command to the disciples "not to tell anyone about him" just verses before. The very ones closest to Jesus had to hold in tension a painful truth: Jesus was the Messiah and the Son of Man must suffer, be rejected, be killed, and only then rise again. The world would witness the latter, only they would know the former until the third day and beyond. Such truth is hard to handle. Peter's rejection of Jesus' dark declaration was understandable.

I remember being the bearer of tragic news. A terrible car accident had resulted in the death of two people beloved by the person I had to inform of their untimely death. I dreaded making the call. I resolved to be as straightforward as possible, fearing I'd lose my nerve if I said more than: "Jim and Susan are dead." The words tumbled out and the person who loved them deeply said: "No. No they are not dead. No, no, no!" I knew the harsh truth, and yet I had an urge to say in the face of his resolute denial, "Maybe I am wrong, maybe they are alive." I wanted to be relieved of the responsibility of this truth. But I couldn't be. I had been entrusted with a brutal truth that had to be shared openly; anything less would have been cruel. Sometimes, when we are close to people, we are given the sacred trust of holding and sharing horrific truths. We are then called to remain with those left to live in a new, never before imagined reality.

The disciples knew the truth: Jesus was the Messiah. The Son of Man would suffer greatly, be rejected, killed, and then three days later, rise again. Not everyone is entrusted with this truth, not yet, only those closest to Jesus. Peter cried: "No. No you don't. No, no, no!" But Jesus refused to give into Peter's need to soften the painful reality.

Jesus then turned to the crowd and with his disciples told them: "If any want to become my followers, let them deny themselves and take up their cross and follow me. For those who want to save their life will lose it, and those who lose their life for may sake, and for the sake of the gospel will save it." I try to imagine the crowd's response. I try to imagine my own response, as if this were the first time I'd heard Jesus' proclamation. I would like to think I would have been all in — yes, Jesus, I will follow you to the cross, lose my life for you, do whatever is required for the sake of your gospel, not matter the cost. I'd like to think that now, too. I know better.

My words and my actions and my inactions all scream, "No, no, no!" The truth is too difficult. I can't stay with Jesus now that I know what he must endure and what is required of me as his friend and follower. I recently heard a person lament that one of the many losses of a major illness she endured was the loss of close friends. As she underwent painful procedures and treatments, her life hanging in the balance, they disappeared, unable to face the truth that she might die, unable to face the truth that if she, their peer, might die, they might, too. They rebuked her and said: "No! No, no, no!"

Jesus said plainly what he would undergo and clearly defined what was required of his followers. He knew many would not be able to handle the reality of suffering, death, and loss. Many would rebuke him, turn away, and abandon him. Many still do.

That is why Jesus said these things quite openly: suffering, rejection, death, cross bearing, life-losing — these are the truths that accompany the Son of Man. On the third day Jesus will rise again. Those who lose their lives for the sake of the gospel will save them; this is the truth that comes with following Christ, too. Can we hold these realities in tension? Are we able to bear the suffering long enough to witness resurrection?

My college-age son called me to tell me he had gone to an Ash Wednesday service. (I think he wanted full credit.) He went to a service that was not Presbyterian, and he recounted the differences. The one that struck him the most was that at the imposition of ashes he was not told, "You are dust and to dust you shall return." Instead he heard,

"Repent, and turn to the gospel." He relayed a sense of disappointment. He was seeking the definitive declaration of his finitude. He went to hear a truth, a brutal truth, told plainly and openly, and anything less seemed disingenuous.

We need to hear openly — from Jesus and in church — the truth of suffering, rejection, and death. That reality surrounds us everywhere else, doesn't it? Jesus entrusts us with the truth of his messiahship, the cross and resurrection. We must hear the whole truth if we are to stay the course and follow Jesus. We must hear the whole truth if we are to stay with those who suffer here and now. We must hear the whole truth if we are to lose our lives for the sake of the gospel.

Time and time again I want to scream, "No! No, no, no!" in the face of yet another school shooting, and another friend's cancer diagnosis, and the scourge of addiction, poverty, and war. I want to turn aside, run away, and pretend that these brutal realities are fake news. It is only in rare moments of faithful courage, when I hear Jesus speak the whole truth: The Son of Man must undergo great suffering, be rejected, killed and rise on the third day. If you want to follow me, take up your cross, lose your life with me, for me and be saved.

We are dust and to dust we shall return, but we sing alleluia as we go to the grave because we know the truth — the whole brutal, beautiful truth of our Messiah, the Son of Man, the one we follow to the cross, the resurrected one who comes to us despite our rebukes, denials and abandonment. Yes. Yes, yes, yes.

This week:

- Have you ever experienced the abandonment of friends during a difficult time? Were there people who remained with you no matter what you were facing? What was that like?

- Why do you think Jesus tells the disciples not to share that he is the Messiah, but says openly that he will suffer and be killed?

- Imagine hearing Jesus' declaration that you must lose your life for him and the sake of the Gospel as if for the first time.

What is your reaction? What does it mean to lose your life for Jesus and for the sake of the gospel?

- What does it mean to "take up your cross?" Are you taking up your cross?
- How do we gain the world and forfeit our lives?
- As Lent progresses, how are your Lenten practices going? What are you learning about yourself? Your faith? God?

## Third Sunday in Lent
Exodus 20:1-17; I Corinthians 1:18-25; John 2:13-22

Jesus, early in his ministry in John's gospel, ventures to Jerusalem for the festival of Passover. He will, of course, be in Jerusalem again, near the end of his ministry and his life.

The synoptic gospels have Jesus in Jerusalem for Passover once, where he cleansed the temple shortly before his arrest and death. Not so for John. The cleansing of the temple took place in chapter two, just after he performed his first sign in Cana of turning water into wine, long before his final meal with his closest friends. The newly-called disciples got a glimpse of an angry, unyielding Jesus who spoke truth to power from the onset of his mission. No gentle, lamb-carrying Savior here. I wonder if the whip-of-cords, table-turning Jesus was frightening or if it thrilled them?

I admit that a part of me pumps my fist at the thought of Jesus giving those vendors what they have coming to them. You show them, Jesus! God's house is not a ritual Walmart. Religious festivals are not about blow-up yard art, over-the-top gift-giving, chocolate bunnies, or expensive new clothes. Give 'em hell, Jesus! Put God back in Passover. I want to channel temple-cleansing Jesus every time I hear of churches fighting about the color of the carpet, blessing guns, closing their doors to the poor, or announcing that some tragedy is a result of some community's sin. The house of God cannot be co-opted for our human purposes and our propensity for greed, exploitation, and self-righteousness. Crack the whip, Jesus!

The problem, of course, with this line of thinking is that in every scenario listed above I am on the handle-end of the whip. I am helping Jesus turn over others' tables, pouring out those sinners' coins, and holding up the sign that indicts those who desecrate God's house. In short, I cast myself as Jesus — not disciple, not wrong-hearted religious leader, not wrong-headed purveyor of doves. Whenever I want to cast myself in the role that can only be occupied by the Son of God, I need to stop, drop, and repent. I need to repeat until I believe it: *I — am — not — Jesus!*

I am not one with the Father as Jesus is. I am not the temple that will be destroyed and raised in three days. I am not seated at the right hand of the Father, judge of the quick and the dead. On any given occasion I am a disciple, a Pharisee and/or a defiler of the holy. On every given occasion, I am a sinner, always in need of table-turning Jesus to come and set me right.

The temptation to use this text to justify our righteous indignation is strong. I want Jesus to set straight those I deem in the wrong. In order to not give into that temptation, I must first recognize the ways I have sullied God's dwelling places in sanctuary, self, and world.

Lent demands that we examine how we have desecrated the divine by selling out the Holy Spirit through the sacrificial dove trade. How have we used the temple as a means of personal profit rather than a place of worship? When have we wrapped our preferences in the packaging of the faith, instead of examining our practices through the lens of Jesus Christ? What have we placed ahead of God?

As soon as we want to grab the whip of cords from Jesus' hand, we need to stop, drop, and repent because, odds are, we are no less in need of radical purification and reorientation than the ones we wish to condemn.

The gospel lesson for this week is coupled with Exodus 20:1-17: the Ten Commandments. Note the "I am" and "you shall" and "you shall not" language. "I am the Lord your God… you shall have no other gods before me." "I am the Lord your God… you shall not make for yourself an idol." You shall remember the sabbath and honor your father and mother. The covenant sets out the relationship, the order, the responsibilities. Worship of God comes first and any practice that disputes that priority creates the occasion for Jesus to come and turn the tables on us.

Before we cheer on Jesus as he went to town on those who made God's house a marketplace, or give in to the temptation to cast ourselves as Jesus, we need to ask for the Spirit's intercession and intervention so that we might get our own house in order, personally and corporately. Bryan Stevenson, the Harvard-trained public defense lawyer, author of "Just Mercy" and founder of the Equal Justice Initiative was recently interviewed for "Pacific Standard Magazine". Stevenson talked about the need to get in proximity to have a lasting and meaningful impact for good. He said he sees many people who "feel very comfortable challenging other people and holding other people accountable." But he went on to add, "I think it's necessary that it be disconnected from a sense of privilege because too often people who are willing to participate in a sit-in or to engage in counter-protests or to participate in a demonstration are not willing to actually serve the poor. They're not willing to pursue a career that creates proximity to the systems we are so provoked by. And I want to make sure that we understand that what you do for a couple of hours is not going to negate what you do for a lifetime, if what you do for a lifetime is adding to the problem."

It feels so good to crack the whip, turn the tables, and rail against those who get religion so wrong. But doing so has no lasting impact on that which so provokes us if we are unwilling to see how we are contributing to the defacing of the divine in our own lives and houses of worship. We must get in proximity to and ferret out whatever exists within and around us, that transforms dwelling places of the holy into spaces uninhabitable for God.

We must remember as we do so that Jesus doesn't crack the whip and move on, he returns to Jerusalem for yet another Passover: the one where the temple of his body will be destroyed, giving his life so that the tables will be turned forever and finally on sin and death. Forgiveness, reconciliation, redemption and resurrection are coming for wrong-hearted, wrong-headed, dove-selling sinners.

This week:

- Look at where the account of the cleansing of the temple is placed in Mark, Matthew, and Luke. Where is it found in the narrative? What is significant about John's placement of the story at the beginning of Jesus' ministry?

- Jesus in this text does not debate, discuss or offer the possibility for people to repent and stop what they are doing. Is this troubling? Are there occasions where God simply says, "No more"?
- The people selling animals for sacrifice in the temple likely thought they were providing a needed service. Are there ways we mask idolatry with faithful service?
- What is the role of righteous indignation in a life of faith? How do we act on it without making ourselves the judge or even Jesus?
- In verse 22, John noted that after Jesus was raised from the dead, the disciples remembered what Jesus said about the temple being destroyed and raised. We are told in Exodus to remember the sabbath. What is the role of scripture in remembering rightly and understanding the present?
- How might you use this season of Lent to discern the tables Jesus needs to turn in your life? In other words, what needs to be cleansed in order to make way for the holy?

## Fourth Sunday in Lent

Numbers 21:4-9; Ephesians 2:1-10; John 3:14-21

John 3:16. Even in this age when education through memorization has fallen out of favor, many Christians know this verse by heart.

In a church I served, every elementary-aged Sunday school student was required to recite this verse from memory. (One student, I am told, insisted on doing so while standing on his head. But, he got the job done.) John 3:16. Printed on shopping bags of some retailers, held up on posters at sporting events, embossed on vanity car license plates in every state — John 3:16.

"For God so loved the world, that he gave his only Son, that whoever believes in him should not perish but have eternal life." The gospel in one verse, right? A lovely encapsulation of the character of God and the work of Jesus Christ. Much catchier than say, John 3:14: "And as Moses lifted up the serpent in the wilderness, so much the Son of Man be lifted up." Much more inclusive sounding than John 3:18: "Whoever believes in him is not condemned, but whoever does not believe is condemned already, because they have not believed in the name of the only Son of God." Much more encouraging than John 3:19: "And this is the judgment: the light has come into the world, and the people loved the darkness rather than the light because their works were evil."

Isolating each verse makes it clear why John 3:16 gets the airtime that some of the others in this reading don't. Although a case could be made for John 3:17: "For God did not send his Son into the world to condemn the world, but in order that the world might be saved through him." Perhaps not as concise, but it still packs a theological punch.

But if we take John 3:16 (or any verse) in isolation, we lose the fullness of God's Word to us. I would also argue that in our time, emblazoning John 3:16 on poster, bag, or billboard means little to nothing. Who is John? What do those numbers represent? Even printing the verse out doesn't help much as in our post-pluralistic society; people are not waking up at night wrestling with matters of eternal life. I am not sure that those in our pews are often wringing their hands or clutching their pearls over the matter, either. The state of our present world, yes. Their status in eternity, not so much.

But this is exactly where expanding beyond John 3:16 speaks a timeless and timely word. How about this for resonance? "People loved darkness rather than the light because their works were evil. For everyone who does wicked things hates the light and does not come to the light, lest their works should be exposed." The language of evil and wicked may not make the headlines, but wicked deeds and their evil results sure do.

Here is a quick sampling from today's headlines as I write this reflection:

"Conviction in fatal school bathroom attack overturned"
"Parents arrested after three children found living inside box for years"
And I haven't clicked on the "global news" tab yet.
People love darkness more than light because their works were evil.

This is the world God so loves. That's the shocking truth of John 3:16-17. God so loves *this* world, filled to overflowing with evil works and darkness. God loves this world so much that God sent the Son of Man, God's Son, not to condemn it, but to save it.

This week while traveling, I took a walk around the neighborhood near my hotel. I walked past a Home Depot where a large group of men were standing, waiting, hoping, to get picked up to work for the day. I walked passed a person with a cardboard sign asking for help on not one corner, but at every intersection. I witnessed a person defecating by the side of the road and while, at first, I confess, I was disgusted, upon reflection I was deeply saddened. How do we live in a culture that denies people the dignity of an accessible bathroom? I said out loud to myself as I walked, "God, we aren't doing such a good job here." I really thought, "God, how do you love this world?" There are days I certainly don't. Days where I witness people who are truly loving the darkness, exploiting the poor, abusing the vulnerable, pushing aside the weak, ridiculing the different, laughing at those who suffer.

Then I read John 3:16: "For God so loved the world, that he gave his only Son, that whoever believes in him should not perish but have eternal life."

And John 3:17: "For God did not send his Son into the world to condemn the world, but in order that the world might be saved through him."

This world. God loves *this* world. God chooses not to condemn *this* world. God desires salvation, life eternal, and abundance for *this* world. And if we love the light more than the darkness, we are called to desire those very things for this world, too.

That's the call for those of us who have accepted that God's Son, was given for ALL. This requires entering those places of deep darkness, not turning away from them.

It isn't enough to hold up posters, or put a bumper sticker on our car, or memorize the verse. We who were once dead in sin are now alive together with Christ — not through our own doing, but through God's power and grace — are "created in Christ Jesus for good works" and must walk in those good works, especially in places of darkness and evil.

The gift of God's eternal life and love is just that, a gift — one that we receive and do not earn. We, too, love the dark and have no shortage of evil deeds on our cosmic resume. And yet, God so loves the world, so loves each and all of us, that the Son of Man, God's own son, comes to save, not condemn. The judgment is this: whether we turn toward the light or away from it, whether we reflect it or hide it, whether we become a beacon or a stumbling block, whether we follow the light and walk in good works or huddle on the sidelines waiting to pounce on the vulnerable. In short, do our lives reveal the truth that God so loves the world or do we, through our deeds, condemn it?

God so loves *this* world. Do we?

This week:

- What does eternal life mean in John's gospel? If John has a "realized eschatology," what are the implication of God's gift of eternal life here and now?

- Why do people love the darkness more than light? What is appealing about the darkness?
- When you think about God's judgment, do you think about John 3:19? If not, what biblical verses or stories do you think about? How do they differ or resonate with John 3:19?
- Read the text from Numbers appointed for this Sunday. Notice how Moses advocates for the very people who have complained against him. What can we learn from Moses in this story?
- Ephesians 2:10 says we are God's "workmanship." What does that mean? What would it look like if we were to think of ourselves in this way?
- It is the fourth week of Lent. How are your Lenten practices going? What have you learned? Any insights you have gleaned?

## Fifth Sunday in Lent
John 12:20-33 (34-36)

Some Greeks wanted to see Jesus.

They must have heard stories about Jesus. Word had gotten around about this Jesus who had brought a man back from the dead. Maybe one of the Greeks was a friend of a friend who knew the man born blind who could now see. Maybe they were even members of the crowd who'd waved palm tree branches called, "Hosanna!" Maybe they simply wondered what all the hype was about, and they wanted to see for themselves if there was anything to the wild stories about this man called Jesus.

They knew enough, these Greeks, to know that Philip is one of Jesus' followers, so they went to him and said, "Sir, we wish to see Jesus." A simple, straightforward request: We wish to see Jesus.

Philip — the one with a Greek name, the one Jesus asked to feed the 5,000, the one who invited Nathanael to "come and see" for himself that this man from Nazareth is indeed the one about whom Moses and the prophets wrote — goes to Andrew, and the two of them go to Jesus.

"Jesus, there are some Greeks who've requested to see you." Philip and Andrew told him.

"The hour has come for the Son of Man to be glorified," Jesus said, and then used the metaphor of a single kernel of wheat dying and bearing fruit. He went on to say that those who love their life will lose it, and added a bit about following him and serving him and the Father honoring those who followed and served him.

Huh?

"But, Jesus, some Greeks want to see you. Is that a yes or a no? What do you want us to tell them?"

Jesus went on with one of those Johannian monologues: "My soul is troubled. What should I say? 'Father save me from this hour?' No, this hour is the very reason I have come. Father, glorify your name."

Then the voice from heaven chimed in about having already glorified and will glorify again — and some thought it was thunder and some thought an angel had spoken and still, somewhere, some Greeks were waiting, wanting to see Jesus, and Philip, and Andrew were wondering what to do. Maybe those Greeks heard the voice that Jesus said was for the sake of the crowd, or maybe they didn't. The focus had shifted, and Jesus went back and forth with those crowded around him discussing whether the Messiah remained forever. Another question was posed by the crowd that maybe included some Greeks: "Who is this Son of Man?"

That seemed pretty straight forward. Couldn't Jesus have said, "Me. I am the Son of Man"?

But he instead went into another metaphor, not of/about grain or wheat, but light: walk in the light, believe in the light, become children of the light.

Huh? Is that a yes or a no? Are you, or aren't you? What does it mean that the Father's name has been and will be glorified? Can't we just see Jesus?

Well that depends, because seeing in John's gospel goes deeper than visual sight. Those who truly could see recognized the truth that was elusive to others. Those who saw in John's gospel believed. Those who saw in John's gospel recognized the connection between Jesus and the Father. Those who saw Jesus in John's gospel knew who Jesus really was and followed. But what Jesus said — his talk of the grain falling to the ground and dying to bear fruit, his declaration about being raised up, his call again to choose light over darkness — invited the crowd, the Greeks and Jews, disciples and palm-wavers, to reconsider what seeing him meant.

Seeing Jesus, in John's sense of seeing, is believing, following, serving, dying to an old life and being raised to a new one. Do you really want to see Jesus?

Throughout the gospel, Jesus had encounters with those who were curious or those who were in need, people who thought they wanted to see Jesus: Nicodemus, the rich young ruler, the royal official, crowds, the man born blind. But not all of them, once they learned what seeing

Jesus entailed, wanted to see him clearly enough to do what was required and follow.

For John, seeing Jesus is believing, believing is following, and following is dying to self in order to be reborn. Not everyone really wants that kind of sight.

At this point in John's gospel, Jesus was in Jerusalem to celebrate his final earthly Passover. He had entered the city to face the hour of glory that comes before his death and resurrection. The time for curiosity had run out, the time for commitment was at hand. Jesus wanted to know if some Greeks and the crowd and the disciples really saw him, the Son of Man, who would die and be raised for the sake of them all.

Curiosity about signs and wonders is easy. Commitment to follow, no matter the circumstances, is hard. Jerusalem is the place where the choice between those two stances must be made. Do you really want to see Jesus?

In this season of much rhetoric and many causes, it is easy to be curious, to go from one headline to the next, one rant and diatribe to the next. But to what — no, to whom — are we truly committed and willing to stand with, no matter the cost? For what — no, for whom — are we willing to lose our lives?

Like many, I have been outraged and heartbroken about the latest mass shooting. I have prayed. I attended a workshop on preventing gun violence. I have reached out to friends further along the path in advocating for changes in policy and laws. I have been working on ways I can leverage my sphere of influence to make a difference. But I realized that I had not fully committed because I had not seen, really seen, the human cost of this violence. I came to this revelation when I read this article in Buzzfeed, "This is what a fourteen-year-old girl left behind after she died in a mass shooting." (https://www.buzzfeednews. com/article/remysmidt/alyssa-alhadeff-parkland-victim-bedroom#. cal7AXxmvO)

I read: "Alyssa's room was full of signs of high school life and remained as she left it. Textbooks were strewn about the floor, as were notecards, hairbrushes, markers. On her dresser there were face masks (which she loved) along with a box of nail polish." The paragraphs of text were interrupted by images of a soccer jersey, a sparkly dress, and hairbrushes. I wept as I read and scrolled. I have a fourteen-year-old daughter, and a seventeen-year-old one too. I pictured their rooms: the nail polish, the snow globes, the posters, the books, and the facemasks. I saw the events of February 14, 2018 in a way that I had not seen them before, in a way I could subsequently never *unsee,* and the right response to truly seeing is commitment. Half-hearted curiosity would be an abomination.

Do we really want to see Jesus?

This week:

- What do "glory" and "glorify" mean in this text? What do we mean when we talk about glory? How do the two meanings relate (or not)?
- Where are the other places in scripture where a heavenly voice is heard? What is the message of those passages? Why do you think some people heard thunder and others an angel? Were there some who didn't hear it at all?
- Look at other passages in John's gospel where people sought out Jesus. What were they looking for from him? What happens once they encountered him?
- In verse 32, Jesus said that he would be lifted up and draw all people to himself. What did you make of the word "all"? Does "all" really mean "all?"
- Why did Philip go get Andrew before he went to tell Jesus about the request of "some Greeks?"
- We are well into Lent. How are your Lenten practices going? What have you learned? What questions have they raised for you?

Palm/Passion Sunday

Mark 11:1-11

Why are you doing this? What are you doing?

These two questions are front and center in Mark's version of Jesus' entry into Jerusalem. We could add a few more questions from the other gospel accounts of this story. Matthew asked: Who is this? Luke's version posits a specific query: Why are you untying the colt? John didn't ask questions so much as state the disciples' ongoing confusion: "His disciples did not understand these things at first; but when Jesus was glorified, then they remembered that these things had been written of him and had been done to him." John's gospel must always be read back to front. But Mark emphasized basic human curiosity: Why are you doing this? What are you doing? It's the bystanders who ask the disciples as they were untying the colt, "What are you doing?"

The disciples did as they were told and relayed the message Jesus instructed them to share: "The Lord needs it and will send it back here immediately." The colt was on loan for a specific, ritual task. Not unlike the silver communion ware that is polished, passed, and returned to the locked cabinet, needed for a particular, holy function, borrowed not kept. These bystanders, whoever they were, "allow them to take it," trusting Jesus and his followers at their word.

Why are you doing this? What are you doing? These seem reasonable questions for crowds, bystanders and disciples alike to ask of Palm and Passion Sunday. We must look an odd sight to those passing by our sanctuaries on Sunday morning as we stand outside with palm branches, some of us dressed in our finest and others in robes, children roaming, youth huddling, all ages gathering to sing and process. Anyone unfamiliar with what week it is (and many will have no idea what week it is on the liturgical calendar) might ask: Why are you doing this? What are you doing?

Most of the world will know what the signs and the march the day before this day are about. I am writing thhis as many gather for a protest march against gun violence. Even those who vehemently disagree with the premise and proposed policies of March for Our Lives know the why: Parkland, Newtown, Columbine. It would be difficult for anyone not completely off the grid to miss the what: a march to end gun violence in schools and communities. But this Sunday's procession around the neighborhood or inside the sanctuary, coupled with palm branches and hymns — not poster boards, speeches, and chants — begged the questions from crowds, bystanders, and some confused disciples: Why are you doing this? What are you doing?

Can we answer those questions, should anyone care to ask us? Shouldn't we be able to say: Jesus told us to relay this message to anyone who asks: 'This is for the Lord'? "The Lord is coming into our cities and towns, our sanctuaries, and our streets." That's why we are doing this. We are preparing for his entry into the midst of chaos, crowds, killers, suffering, and exploitation. That's what we are doing.

Saturday's march against gun violence was not untethered from Sunday's procession for Jesus, no matter where you stand on kids walking out or walking up, bump stocks, assault weapons, or background checks. Jesus' entry into Jerusalem is Jesus' entry into Washington and Parkland, Newtown and Columbine, Aleppo and Ferguson, Charlottesville and St. Louis, or Kabul and Taiz. Jesus is coming to all the places in desperate need of him — the places and the people who need to know that the Prince of Peace, Son of David, is the priest with the power to heal, the prophet who brought God's justice and the king who is rules both heaven and earth.

What are you doing? We are waving palms and singing hosanna, welcoming the Lord, prophet, priest, and king, who is coming into our streets, on the way to the cross, to turn the current world order upside down.

Why are you doing this? Because we want to follow Jesus and be part of the new, life-giving, creation-redeeming thing God is doing through him.

Jesus is Lord of all. What we do on Sunday cannot be extricated from marches on Saturday or our actions on Monday. The one who enters Jerusalem, humble and on a donkey, is the very one who will take on the sin of the world, be executed, die and be buried, raised from the grave and ascend into heaven, to judge the living and the dead. Nothing is off limits to our Lord. That's why we do what we do on Palm Sunday, Maundy Thursday, Good Friday, and Easter Sunday and every Sunday afterward. We make public our loyalty and our love for Jesus Christ, and our commitment to follow the Lord of all, every day, everywhere, anywhere.

Palm branches are not as explicit to the world as poster board, but we are a far more powerful force for transformation when we recognize the what and why of our waving them this week.

The Lord, the prophet who rides the ritually pure colt, is the culminating call of God's cries for justice on behalf of the oppressed. He is the king, anointed by cloak and the crowd's declaration who rules heaven and earth. He is the priest, called Son of David, who has shown relentless mercy. This Lord — our Lord — is entering our streets, our towns, our sanctuaries, our lives to turn the world upside down, and save it — and we want to testify to this truth.

Our parades of leaves and choruses of hosannas pale in scale to the louder, larger gatherings we see on the news, but this Sunday, this week, makes all the other demonstrations penultimate. God will have the last word and when we wave our branches and warble our hymns, we are declaring our allegiance to that word and no other.

It is our allegiance, total and ultimate, that leads us back into the very streets where we lauded Jesus. Washington. Newtown. Columbine. Aleppo. Charlottesville. Schools. Hospitals. Prisons. Homes. Any place or person in need of the saving grace, compassionate mercy, healing justice, and transformative love of God made known to us through our Lord. That's why we are doing this. That's what's at stake. That's the meaning of our palms, cloaks, colts, choruses, and lives.

This week:

- If someone were to ask you about Palm Sunday or Holy Week, "Why are you doing this?" how would you answer?

- Note the connections in the Mark text to other scripture passages that mark Jesus' identity as prophet, priest, and king. For example, read Zechariah 14:4 and 9:9; 1 Samuel 1:6:7; 2 Kings 9:13; and Mark 10:47. What do we learn about Jesus when we think about him in these three ways?

- Read the accounts of Jesus' entry into Jerusalem in the other three gospels: Matthew 21:1-9; Luke 19:28-38; and John 12:12-16. What is distinct about each account? What, do you think, is significant about those distinctions?

- What Christian practices do we do that cause others to be curious and ask, "What are you doing?" or "Why are you doing this?" Have you ever had someone ask you about your Christian practices?

- Notice how Jesus asks for things from people that have them: a colt, a spare room, and so on. Can you think of other biblical examples of Jesus asking to use something for his purposes? What were those things? What did Jesus do with them? What might Jesus be asking of from you?

- Where are you called to follow Jesus this week? What will it require of you?

## Maundy Thursday

Exodus 12:1-4, (5-10), 11-14; 1 Corinthians 11:23-26;
John 13:1-17, 31b-35

Growing up, I loved Maundy Thursday worship. Going to church in the evening marked the event as special. Communion, being celebrated quarterly in my small town southern church, always garnered my attention. The table looked lovely with silver trays and white, embroidered cloth. As a child, the small pieces of bread and the tiny cups reminded me of my doll house; everything miniature and neat, one of the few times something in the sanctuary felt made for me.

I think, although I cannot be certain, I partook of the bread and cup for the first time on a Maundy Thursday. At that time, church policy did not allow children to come to the table until after they went through the confirmation process and, if I recall rightly, those classes took place in the new calendar year. Hence, our first opportunity to receive the elements came on Maundy Thursday. Specialness and mystery surrounded the service, and ever since I have made it a point to go to church on Maundy Thursday. Even in those college years when darkening the door of a sanctuary rarely occurred, I would make my way to some church, somewhere, to hear once again Jesus' new commandment, embodied in his willingness to wash the disciples' feet.

I had heard this passage from John while sitting in a Presbyterian pew year after year, and while each occasion coincided with the Lord's Supper, never did we enact the foot washing part of the passage. We just did not do that in my tradition, at least not then. Honestly, I did not know it was an option. I did not know that in other parts of Christ's Body, every Maundy Thursday included not only communion, but foot washing as well. I did not know this until I married an Episcopalian and ended up worshiping with him in that tradition for a season.

I loved our little Episcopal communion. Quirky described our gatherings. Causal dress, formal liturgy. All manner of people present whenever the doors opened. Occasionally, someone wandered into the middle of the service and walked out whenever the Spirit, or something else, moved them. Despite the laid back ethos of the congregation, holy week services were carefully planned events that included musicians, artists, smells, bells and every available liturgical accessory. Without question, Maundy Thursday would entail foot washing.

Foot washing. The mere thought of such an intimate act in a public space made my Presbyterian sensibilities go on high alert. How, I wondered, does this even work? Do we wash one another's feet? Does the priest do all the scrubbing? How much water is involved? What shoes does one wear? I pestered my husband who was bemused by my anxious questions. For him, such a happening in church seemed normal — expected — not at all noteworthy. He had a point, of course: all those years of hearing the text, Jesus did say we ought to wash one another's feet. Like too many of Jesus' admonitions, I did not take it literally.

Maundy Thursday arrived. I donned what I hoped were the correct shoes, opting for sandals, thinking no socks was a practical and time saving choice. As the service moved forward, I found my anxiety rising. Finally, the priest stood, put a towel over his shoulder and made his way around the room. Ours was a small group and the space arranged with chairs in a circle. He knelt in front of each of us in turn, moving the small basin of water with him. All was silent, save the gentle splash of water and the rustling of the priestly robe as he moved from one person to the next. The act itself proved to be brief and simple, and what happened at the end moved me deeply. Just as the priest completed the circle and went to continue the liturgy, someone among us stopped him, invited him to sit and washed the priest's feet. No one would leave without receiving this tangible service of grace.

I have now experienced foot washing services numerous times, and each occasion uncovers profound meaning in simple sacred acts. The vulnerability of washing and having one's feet washed reminds me of our real need for one another. The embodied nature of that part of the liturgy reminds me that redemption, worship, salvation, and abundant life encompasses absolutely every part of us. The imagined image of Jesus, on his knees, washing my feet overwhelms me and I can relate to

Peter's shock and dismay. Every single time I remember the first time I participated in a Maundy Thursday foot washing, I am compelled to look around and make sure no one is left out. No one is left out. Perhaps that is the message I most need to know on Maundy Thursday and on Good Friday and on Easter, too. Jesus does not leave anyone out, not even Judas, and therefore, following that new commandment, neither should we.

This week:

- Is foot washing part of your tradition? If not, would you want to experience it? Why or why not?
- If you have participated in foot washing, what was that experience like?
- What are some of your most memorable Maundy Thursday worship services? What made them so?
- When you think about Jesus' new commandment to love one another, how do you connect it with the sacraments? With foot washing?
- Jesus says the world will know we are his followers by our love for one another. Does the world look at us and know we follow Jesus?
- What tangible acts of service have you done or received in Jesus' name?

## Good Friday
Isaiah 52:13-53:12; Hebrews 10:16-25; John 18:1-19:42

When do we talk about abandonment, despair, and suffering in the sanctuary or Sunday school classrooms of our churches? When do we lament like the psalmist, or complain bitterly like some of the prophets or murmur our confusion over God's plan like the Israelites in the desert? Somehow, our services got sanitized and we come to worship in our literal or metaphorical "Sunday best." We appear to have it all together even when inside we are utterly shattered. Now, this may well not be the case in your congregation or tradition. Results may vary. However, for many Christians, we interpret faithfulness as feigning feeling good rather than brining our whole, messy, wounded selves to God and putting everything at the feet of Jesus, at the foot of the cross.

Good Friday is that rare day on the liturgical calendar when weeping and grief, sorrow and doubt, brokenness and confusion, refuse to be silenced. Whether at noon or after the sun sets, we gather and hear John's passion narrative read, in full, and sit with the magnitude of the Son of Man, who was betrayed, abused, and murdered. We depart without greeting each other in the narthex or shaking the hand of the preacher at the door. No words. No platitudes. No reassuring hymns. No beloved verse of scripture offered as a Band-Aid on the gaping injuries of this world or our souls.

This is why we need Good Friday. We need assurance that our God knows the depths of human cruelty, violence, and pain. We need to see how fully human Jesus endured all we could possibly face and refused to take a divine out, but instead, tended to his devastated mother, welcomed a reprobate criminal into the kingdom and uttered forgiveness with his next to last breath. There is nowhere we can go, nothing we can experience that is godforsaken. Jesus redeemed it all and Good Friday confirms this unshakable, gospel truth.

Every Good Friday, Christians are given the gift of witnessing God's relentless, total commitment to save us, to be with us, to reconcile with us and each other. This gift comes in an ugly package. The gift of imagining the horror of the cross is not one we always want to accept. We, like those first disciples, often give into temptations to turn or run away. However, if we are able to remain, we learn the lengths God will go to be in relationship with us and this fallen world. We see that nothing, no one, is godforsaken. Jesus did not turn away from even the most debase within or around us. We can trust his promised presence to never abandon or leave us orphaned.

Good Friday worship is markedly different than almost any other service in that it faces the evil head-on in the world and the times it feels as if darkness overwhelms the divine good of all creation. We know the rest of the story. We understand that Easter is coming and that evil's victory is temporary, even though it feels total. Nonetheless, Good Friday affords us the opportunity to feel, without shame or embarrassment, despair, sorrow, hopelessness, grief, loss, and the entire gambit of emotions that too often we leave in the narthex of the sanctuary.

In a world where we turn away from suffering, Good Friday reminds us that God enters into it in order to defeat sin and overcome death. Good Friday reminds us, therefore, that we too can stand with the afflicted and trust that Jesus is there with us working for good.

On this sorrowful day, bring your whole self and all the complex, chaotic, huge needs of the world into the sanctuary. Do not turn away. Look fully upon Jesus on the cross. Then set your burdens down there, knowing he takes them all, and through his death and soon-to-come-resurrection, he will redeem them.

This week:

- Do you feel as if you must bring your "best self" to church? Why or why not?
- When have you expressed or shared painful emotions or experiences in your faith community? How did others respond to you?
- Why do you think Good Friday worship is important?
- What are some memorable Good Friday services you have experienced? What made them so?

- Do you find it difficult to be with those in pain or to go to places where there is suffering? How can you stay with those in those circumstances?
- Read several of the gospel passion narratives. What stands out the most to you?

## Resurrection of the Lord
## Mark 16:1-8

Secrets people take to the grave don't often stay there.

Movies, reality television, and soap operas make great use of secrets long buried coming back to life and rendering the living shocked, distressed or utterly amazed. The long-lost heir to the fortune who was thought dead crashes the family reunion. The man he knew as Dad, it turns out, was not his biological father. The reason the family immigrated was to seek a new life… but the backstory involved fleeing from the law. Lo and behold, the results from the DNA kit that got mailed off reveal an entirely unexpected family heritage. Grave secrets from one generation come back to life, no matter how silent the witnesses to them remained. How is that possible when the parties involved are dead and buried?

Secrets people take to the grave don't necessarily stay there. They have a life of their own in family lore, and future generations and communities with a propensity to not mind their own business will surely inquire. Mary Magdalene and Mary the mother of James and Salome fled the tomb in terror and the stranger nearby visiting a spouse's grave got a glimpse of them and wondered what had caused such a reaction. Even though they told "no one nothing" as the Greek in Mark wants to emphasize, there were people in town who wondered about the large stone adjacent to the tomb that it had previously covered.

Mary Magdeline, Mary the mother of James, and Salome were in shock, and who could blame them? Don't the dead stay dead? How many teenage boys in white robes have proclaimed the gospel to you at the graveside? As linguist George Lakoff, quoted in David John Seel Jr.'s book, *The New Copernicans* noted: "People think in frames…. To be accepted, the truth must fit people's frame. If facts do not fit the frame, the frame stays and facts bounce off." If you are coming to anoint a dead body, news of a living person does not fit the frame. No wonder they were distressed, stupefied, and agitated. No wonder they told "no one nothing." Who would have believed them anyway?

And yet, we know the truth that didn't fit their frame — or anyone else's for that matter. Someone, at some point, said something to someone else. Grave secrets have a way of coming back to life and when they do, those who discover them often have to reframe their whole entire lives because all they thought was true, well, wasn't.

That's what Easter does. It reframes absolutely everything when the grave secret comes out.

The three woman talked amongst themselves, and the person at the next table over in the Galilean Starbucks overheard them. Maybe Mary leaned in close to Salome and said, "What did that young man say? Did I hear it right? Jesus, our Jesus, the Jesus of Nazareth, the very one we saw brutally crucified, has been raised? Did he tell us we'd see him in Galilee? Is that what you heard, too?" And Salome nodded solemnly, still afraid. The grave secret started to leak faster than the words of a White House insider to a "Washington Post" reporter.

It is hard to take a secret to the grave because we live in community where people talk — neighbors notice — and privacy then as now is often an illusion. After every tragic headline, the cameras go up and teachers, passersby, and former classmates are asked, "Are you surprised? What did you notice about him or her or them?"

"Well, you know, he kept to himself mostly, but he was a little, I don't know, sort of strange."

"I saw people going in and out at odd hours."

"I wondered why the curtains were always closed."

"Once I saw the police in their driveway."

"As soon as I heard it on the news I thought: It's her. I just knew it."

Secrets don't stay secret very often even when the ones closest to them keep quiet. We don't know what happened next with Mary, Mary, and Salome in Mark's gospel, but we do know the secret they tried to keep did not remain in the grave. We know what that adolescent proclaimed: "Jesus of Nazareth, who was crucified, the one you are looking for, has been raised. You can look all you want in every corner of this tomb, but you won't find him here. Go tell Peter and the disciples that Jesus is going ahead of you to Galilee and he will meet you there, just like he told you."

You came looking through the frame of death, ready to anoint a body, but the fact is, Jesus is alive. Even if you can't grasp it yet, the fact remains: He has been raised. Time to reframe and begin looking for Jesus among the living — not in the graveyard, but in Galilee.

There is a story told about Galileo. It is likely apocryphal, but nonetheless insightful. Forced to recant that the earth moved around the sun, the story went that Galileo said, "And yet it moves." In other words, people's inability to see the truth does not make it any less truthful. Mary, Mary, Salome, and perhaps you and I may be so stupefied, terrified, and flummoxed at life where we expect death that we tell no one anything, but, Jesus has still been raised and that truth will not be squelched.

They said nothing to anyone and yet, Jesus still lives. Thanks be to God that the truth of resurrection that reframes everything is not dependent upon us. No matter what we say, or don't say, this grave secret is no secret at all. This exposed grave secret, in fact, means we no longer need to be afraid of our own secrets, the things we want no one to know, the dead places, pre-dawn worries, shocking, distressing ideas, actions, or attitudes can be buried, dead with Jesus because he has taken our sin to the grave with him. All the burdens and beliefs that have limited the frames of our imaginations and expectations are no match for the truth that Jesus Christ is risen. Death has lost its sting; the redemption of the world has been won, and through our risen Lord all things are possible.

We, with Mary, Mary, and Salome, have heard the news. That teenage boy in white said it plainly: "Jesus of Nazareth, the One who was crucified. He has been raised; he is not here. Look, there is the place they laid him. But go, tell his disciples and Peter that he is going ahead of you to Galilee; there you will see him, just as he told you."

Perhaps that good news is a truth than our current frame cannot handle. That's okay. He still lives. Grave secrets don't stay in the grave and when we are ready to hear them, well, they will reframe everything, and we will no longer be terrified. We will be free.

## Lectionary Reflections

This week:

- Is it significant that the messenger in the tomb is a young man, a youth? Mark mentions a young man in chapter 14:51. Why does the writer of Mark specify the age of this person? Are there youth who are currently proclaiming God's message to the world?

- Have you ever been stupefied or in shock because your expectations were completely turned upside down? Were you able to reframe your expectations?

- The women were concerned about how to roll away the stone at the grave, but they went to anoint Jesus' body anyway. Can you think of examples of people of faith going to serve Jesus despite known obstacles? Have you ever done so? What happened to the "stones" in those instances?

- Mary Magdalene, Mary the mother of James, and Salome are named in Mark 15:40. These women were stalwart and loyal. Can you think of other people in the Bible who demonstrated those characteristics? What about in your life?

- Mark ended with a cliffhanger. Readers are left to wonder what happens next. Does that bother you? Would you have added the longer, later ending if it were up to you?

- What is it that you are too terrified to say to others? Could it be that you need not be afraid?

**Second Sunday of Easter**
Acts 4:32-35; 1 John 1:1-2:2; John 20:19-31

Marks of the resurrected Jesus community or maybe rules for the household of the risen Lord, that's what the texts for this second Sunday of Easter reveal. The fellowship of the One who was raised from the dead looks different from the cultural landscape that surrounded it. Those who have experienced and believed the grave-busting power and love of the Son of God responded with transformed lives. At least, that's what happens in the New Testament.

"Now the whole group of those who believed were of one heart and soul, and no one claimed private ownership of any possession, but everything they owned was held in common."

"We declare to you what we have seen and heard so that you also may have fellowship is with us; and truly our fellowship is with the Father and with his Son Jesus Christ."

"Receive the Holy Spirit. If you forgive the sins of any, they are forgiven them; if you retain the sins of any, they are retained."

"There was not a needy person among them for as many as owned lands or houses sold them and brought the proceeds of what was sold. They laid it at the apostles' feet, and it was distributed to each as any had need."

"If we confess our sins, he who is faithful and just will forgive us our sins and cleanse us from all unrighteousness."

"Peace be with you. As the Father has sent me, so I send you."

According to these passages, this second Sunday of Easter ought to be at least as memorable as last Sunday. The offering ought to be *huge*! The confession sequence might take some significant time, what with all that honest confessing and magnanimous forgiveness happening. Not to mention the rush out the door at the end of the service as everyone scrambles to go where Jesus has sent them. Great grace is going to be exhibited all around, so much so that it will spill out into the streets because the ones who followed Jesus have experienced the miracle of his risen presence, right?

If not, why not? That's a question to be gently raised this week. If our experience of Easter hasn't resulted in a revolutionary change in our hearts, lives, and community, why is that? What are we missing? Do we need some extra proof, like Thomas? That's fair. However, I think Thomas shouldn't be the scapegoat for all doubt and doubters forever and always. I am grateful for his honesty. I'd be upset, too, if I had been the only disciple not present when Jesus walked through the locked doors, exhaled the Holy Spirit and gave all the others his peace. If we are with Thomas this week, that's a faithful place to be.

We may well need reassurance that Jesus truly lives in a world so utterly awash in death, dying, and evil. We may need to ask for some help from our fellow disciples and from God, too. We may need to feel the Spirit's breath on our neck, touch the not-yet-healed wounds of our Savior in order to know for ourselves that the testimony of our friends is indeed true. Jesus doesn't seem to mind making multiple appearances, so it is perfectly reasonable to ask for them. I don't believe Jesus judges our limits. Instead he honors them, even if sometimes we are reluctant to receive that assurance.

So, if you haven't yet been moved to sell your land and give the proceeds to the apostles, or you can't quite forgive a deep hurt you suffered, or accept that you are forgiven for one you inflicted, or you feel overwhelmed not with peace, but with anxiety, Jesus' promise to never leave you abandoned remains true, and the risen Lord makes multiple appearances, and the Holy Spirit still blows where it will. Keep gathering with the disciples. Keep asking to touch the wounded side of your Savior. Keep expecting to see, believe and proclaim, "My Lord and my God!" Faith is not a one-and-done experience, it is a lifelong process.

Maybe your Easter hasn't translated into transformation for other reasons. Maybe you have felt the nudge to let go of that grudge or that property or that worry, but you have resisted because somehow those grudges and those possessions and those obsessions define you or drive you or make you feel strangely comfortable. Maybe the thought of such radical letting go is more terrifying than holding fast to all the things that keep you up at night. Maybe going where Jesus sends you is outside the plans you have for yourself or the expectations of others for you. The ideas of peace, forgiveness, grace, generosity, belief and even radical following are great in theory, but inevitably disruptive in practice. Dead gods don't demand much. The living Lord demands our heart, our soul, our all.

The thing is, however, that it is in the reluctant following, the nascent believing, the faltering forgiving, the mumbled confessing, and the miserly sharing, that the peace of Christ creeps in and the Lord of love breaches barriers and we start to feel something strange stirring our hearts, maybe even the Holy Spirit moving us beyond ourselves and into the world.

We're all Thomas, somewhere between yearning to know and finally believing. We're all hovering between Easter and ordinary time, having glimpsed resurrection but still wondering if it is too good to be true. We're all waffling between forgiveness and resentment, confession and covering up our sin, sharing and hoarding. But living, breathing, took-on-our-sin, defeated-death Jesus walks into all of those in between spaces, even when we padlocked the door. That's the power of God. That's the promise of Jesus Christ. That's the gift of the Holy Spirit. That's the relentless truth of Easter, believe it or not.

So, if the pews are sparse this Sunday, the offering quick to count, the music not as grand and swelling as last week, that's all right. The risen Christ is still in the midst of us, granting us peace, giving us the Holy Spirit and sending us out to forgive, share, extend compassion, and tend to those who have need — in short, sending us to exhibit the marks of the resurrected Jesus so others can see him and believe, too.

This week:

- Read through John 20:19-31 and make note of the gifts Jesus gave his disciples. How have you experienced those gifts?
- Have you ever had a season of deep doubt? A crisis of faith? How did you come to belief again? Or did you?

- When have you experienced radical generosity, either extending or receiving it? What moved you to give? How did it feel to be the recipient of such generosity?
- Jesus said that we are sent no less than God the Father sent him. What does that mean for you? For your community of faith? Where are you supposed to go? What are you to do there?
- Forgiveness is a prominent theme in these Easter texts. Why? How do we practice the forgiveness we are called to extend?
- Does our experience of the risen Christ move us to a radically new lifestyle like it did the early believers in Acts? Should it?

## Third Sunday of Easter
Acts 3:12-19; 1 John 3:1-7; Luke 24:36b-48

Do you know the phrase, "You know better, so do better"? One little girl with whom I am acquainted repeats this phrase with regularity because her mother employs the admonishment in many settings: in church, at the dinner table, after a less-than-stellar report from the teacher, etc. "You know better, so do better." The theory, of course, is that once we possess a certain knowledge, we should employ it. The reality, of course, is often that our knowledge and behavior don't match. Even that pillar of the early church, Paul, confessed, "I do not do the good I want to do, but the evil I do not want to do — this I keep on doing" (Romans 7:19). Knowing, even wanting, to do what is right and good doesn't necessarily mean we actually do so. In fact, sometimes we do the exact opposite. And yet, knowledge seems an irreplaceable part of the equation for living with intentional integrity. Ignorance may be bliss for the one who is ignorant, but those living in the orbit of one who is oblivious may experience things very differently.

Teaching and plain-old Bible study take center stage in the Acts and Luke texts for this third Sunday of Easter. Peter took advantage of the attention he had received from the healing at the beautiful gate and taught. "Why do you wonder at this?" he asked. He connected the dots between Abraham, Isaac, and Jacob — and Jesus. He told the story of Jesus' life, death, and resurrection, implicating his hearers in Jesus' murder. (A bold, rhetorical move.) To which he added this important truth, "I know that you acted in ignorance, as did your rulers." You didn't know better, he said. Further, God fulfilled the prophets in this way, through your ignorance. But now, you know better, Peter told them. You know better, because we — the witnesses to these truths — are teaching, preaching, sharing the story, and filling in the blanks. We are teaching what we've learned so that you, too, can know better and do better. Repent, and be forgiven.

That's the sought response to this lesson: learn and live. Knowledge is power, God's power, if we are willing to act on what we now know.

The risen Christ in Luke's gospel conducts a Bible study, too. The scene is both extraordinary and totally typical for those familiar with Sunday mornings or Wednesday evenings in local congregations. Fallible, more or less faithful, followers of Jesus gather together. Some are more in the know than others. Some are farther along in their faith journey than others. Some are more confident that this gathering will be more meaningful than others. Regardless, they are together; and lo and behold, Jesus showed up, right there in the midst of them. He offered his peace, told them not to be afraid, invited them to touch his hands and feet, and then asked for something to eat. What's a church gathering without food?

Bible study and table fellowship go together. Scripture and snacks are virtually inseparable. Spiritual and physical nourishment go hand in hand. The risen (not a ghost) Jesus, wanted something to eat, and "then he opened their minds to understanding scripture." He went on to tell the story, his story, God's story, now their story too: "It is written, that the Messiah is to suffer and to rise from the dead on the third day, and that repentance and forgiveness of sins is to be proclaimed in his name to all the nations, beginning from Jerusalem. You are witnesses to these things."

Learn and live. You know better, so do better. Knowledge is power, God's power, if you are willing to act out the truth you now know.

Bible study — food — a small gathering of unremarkable people engaging with scripture, telling the story of Jesus' life, death, and resurrection. Listening, wondering, and asking questions. Disciples made open to the possibility that ignorance isn't inevitable, that knowledge of God is joy, and joy is so much better than oblivious, fleeting bliss. Totally typical Sunday school, table conversation, or storytelling made absolutely extraordinary through the power and presence of the risen Christ, the one in our midst whenever two or three are gathered.

"Learn and live," said Peter and the writer of 1 John and our risen, living Lord. We have so often acted out of ignorance. There will often be times when we do not act out what we know. We, like Paul, will do the very things we hate, again and again. But now we know this: the life, death, and resurrection of Jesus Christ enables repentance and the forgiveness of sins. We are witnesses to this. We know it by heart, in our hearts, because we have experienced this amazing grace firsthand. We know that we are to proclaim this truth so that others can learn and live too. Through Jesus Christ and in the words of 1 John we know, "Beloved we are God's children now; what we will be has not yet been revealed. What we do know is this: when he is revealed, we will be like him, for we will see him as he is."

Learn and live. Take claim of the power of this knowledge. Repent. Be forgiven. Just as you have been forgiven, so should you forgive others. Know you are beloved children of God. Tell and teach others this truth to which you are witnesses so that they will come to know they, too, are beloved children of God, forgiven and freed, no longer ignorant but well aware of the presence and power of the most high God.

Hold a typical, extraordinary Bible study in the church, on the streets, at the portico beside the beautiful gate, in the park, at the coffee shop, around your kitchen table. Get people's attention through healing acts of love and service, offer some food, tell the story, the story of Jesus, God's story, our story, the story written and enacted for the sake of all creation. Teach and learn and live. Know better. Do better. Know better. Don't do better. Repent. Repeat. Keep learning, trusting God's promise as told to the prophet Jeremiah, "I will put my law within them, and I will write it on their hearts; and I will be their God, and they shall be my people. No longer shall they teach one another, or say to each other, 'Know the Lord,' for they shall all know me, from the least of them to the greatest, says the Lord; for I will forgive their iniquity, and remember their sin no more."

Such knowledge is too powerful for me and too good to keep to myself.

This week:

- Do you participate in a group Bible study? If so, why? What have you learned?

105

- How do we tell the story of our faith to others? Have you ever shared your faith with others?
- All three of these texts talk about sin, repentance, and forgiveness. Why is this message so primary in post-resurrection stories and the beginnings of the church? Is it still primary for us?
- When have you known better, but not done better? How do we come to act out of what we know?
- Peter seems to honestly, yet graciously, tell his hearers that they have been ignorant. Are we able to do likewise? Has anyone ever corrected your ignorance in a way that was transformative for you?
- Jesus wants to make sure his disciples know that he is not a ghost. What is at stake in his having them touch him and eat with him?

## Fourth Sunday of Easter

Psalm 23; 1 John 3:16-24; John 10:11-18

"I am the Good Shepherd. The Good Shepherd lays down his life for his sheep." No equivocation. No qualifiers. The Good Shepherd lays down his life for the sheep. The Good Shepherd, in contrast to the hired hand, never abandons the flock entrusted to him. The Good Shepherd knows the sheep and the sheep know him. The Good Shepherd described in Ezekiel searches for the sheep, rescues them, gathers them, feeds them, binds up the wounded, and strengthens the weak ones. The Good Shepherd Jesus makes explicit that the flock will expand and the sheep yet to come will be incorporated fully into the flock. No sheep will be left vulnerable to the wolves, uncared for or abandoned.

The image of the Good Shepherd tending to the one beloved flock, so valued and valuable that the shepherd will stop at nothing to keep them gathered and safe, calls forth a longing in me that feels almost primal, mostly subconscious, but unmistakable when I read this passage from John or hear aloud the twenty-third Psalm. I shall not want. Rest will be granted. Fear will be jettisoned for deep contentment. Every threat met with protection, giving way to a sense of deep peace.

I long for the Good Shepherd and I yearn to be part one flock, especially in this season of deep cultural divides. I left a meeting this week, weary of acrimony. The group gathered consists of people of faith. People of faith and of good will, who are committed to working for justice, inclusion, the one beloved flock. And yet, even there, division bordering on disdain could not be avoided. Mostly we are polite, civil, and gentle with one another. Sometimes the center won't hold, however, and frustration mounts and voices grow loud and shrill. The issues brought forth with the raised voices need to be stated, and even when the truth is spoken in love, it is very hard to hear. Some in the group tire of talking and call for action. Others fear acting without conversation leading to consensus will result in more fault lines and less community. More than a few have left the group, not out of malice, but,

I think, out of conflict fatigue. Even a group of good-willed, faithful folks abundantly argue, is it even possible for us to be one flock? Why exert energy trying?

The reality is this: staying at the table is hard. Even if the table is in the presence of friends. At least in the presence of our enemies, we know with whom we are supposed to disagree. After meetings like the one I attended this week, I cannot help but wonder if the wounded to whom the shepherd tends were hurt by a fellow member of the flock. Sometimes the sheep have wolves' clothing and commensurate characteristics. Sometimes even with the best of intentions, we hurt those most in need of care and comfort.

The flock doesn't need protection only from wolves coming from the outside, but also from the other sheep within the pen. Does the Good Shepherd not only stave off wolves but mitigate between competing, ornery, petty, fallible, limited sheep? The comforting word in these shepherd texts. ironically is one of absence. Nowhere does it say that the sheep are well behaved, wise, or worthy of the shepherd's sacrifice. In fact, scripture reveals, as does experience, that those in the flock are prone to wander, greedy, ungrateful, and unlikely to learn from their mistakes. The Good Shepherd lays his life down for them anyway. No equivocations. No qualifiers. The shepherd binds up wounds, inflicted by wolf, flock-mate, circumstances and self alike. That promise keeps me at the table.

The resolute, reliable, compassionate Good Shepherd keeps me at the table, the table that I did not set. The table with guests I did not invite. The table laden with overflowing cups I did not fill. The table where the shepherd gives his body and blood for sinners. The table where Judas sat beside Jesus and Peter did, too. The table where I have denied the host and betrayed him time and time again. The table where the weary gather to lay their burden down for a while. The table where conversation leads to my knowing the ones around it no less than Jesus knows me and them. The table where knowing one another can't help but move us to act, maybe even to the point of laying down our lives for the very ones who sometimes make us want to push back our chairs in anger and bolt. The table where, no doubt, others have struggled to keep company with me as well.

The Good Shepherd doesn't abandon the sheep. The Good Shepherd is always expanding the flock. The Good Shepherd seeks the lost, lonely, frightened, injured, the baffled, bewildered and shocked. The Good Shepherd feeds, binds, and strengthens. The Good Shepherd doesn't assess the sheep's worthiness, but sees each one's God-given belovedness, no matter how they obscure that image in themselves or others. The Good Shepherd sets the table, hosts the dinner, and provides the meal. That's what keeps me at the banquet, even when I know I am not worthy and I wish the shepherd would banish me so that I would no longer yearn for each of us to be more like the divine image buried deep within.

Leaving the table seems so much easier. Feed me to the wolves and let me lament my abandonment. Let everyone fend for themselves so that we don't have the responsibility to care for each other. Instead, the Good Shepherd refuses to give up on me, on you, on the flock. That truth compels me to remember how important this God-centered community is. So important, that Jesus laid down his life for its sake. That reality won't allow me to walk away or allow others to leave so easily.

This week, someone I know, of good will, with a great heart, was deeply hurt by the very person he was striving to help. The wounded, lost sheep he had sought lashed out in fear, frustration, and anger. Isn't that what wounded sheep do? As he recalled the events he was despondent, weary, and ready to abandon the sheep and the flock with which he has been entrusted. But after some reflection, some rest, some green pastures in which to lie down, he resolved to stay at the table with the flock, despite the enemies, the wolves, the valleys, the frustrations, the fear and hurt that inevitably come with living in a community of the wounded, which is all communities. He resolved to stay because he is a follower of the Good Shepherd who laid down his life for the sheep, not because they are worthy, but because they are his and he knows them, and he loves them anyway.

The Good Shepherd who doesn't abandon us strengthens us to not abandon others. The Good Shepherd who give us rest, feeds us, and eats with us, binds up our wounds, he does this so that we can bind the wounds of others with understanding, empathy, and compassion. The Good Shepherd doesn't give up on us. That means, on our good days, we don't give up on each other. And on those days when we simply can't stay a minute longer, when we storm away from the table and say we will never return, that same Good Shepherd goes and seeks us out, gives us rest, and brings us home again.

This week:

- What are the contrasts between the Good Shepherd and the hired hand? Look at other biblical passages about the Good Shepherd and note what makes for a Good Shepherd. For example, Ezekiel 34:11-16, 23.
- Psalm 23 is one of the most familiar and beloved portions of scripture. What memories and feelings does it evoke for you?
- Jesus says that there are more sheep that he will bring to the flock, and that the flock will be one. How do we demonstrate that oneness? (Or not.)
- Have you ever been so frustrated or disillusioned with a community that you left? Is leaving sometimes a faithful choice?
- 1 John says that given that Jesus laid down his life for us, we should do likewise. Do we?
- How do we, as 1 John admonished, "love in truth and action?"

**Fifth Sunday of Easter**
Acts 8:26-40; 1 John 4:7-21; John 15:1-11

Where are the fruitful places for sharing the gospel?

In short, any place where we abide in Jesus. Acts tells us that Philip was sent by an angel of the Lord to the road that went down from Jerusalem to Gaza. "This is a desert road." And yet, even desert roads, when God directs us to them, contain people looking to worship, ready to receive the Word of the Lord, eager to be baptized. Desert roads, when our abiding in Jesus sends us to abide with others, contain water, living water that flows from the believer's heart and is never exhausted.

Good fruit is borne wherever Jesus is present. And when we follow and stay close to Jesus, we bear good fruit, whether on desert roads or city streets. All the appointed texts for this fifth Sunday of Easter invite us to consider what draws us closer to Jesus and what, in contrast, pushes us farther from him. But how do we know which is which? How do we figure out which branches God will throw on the burn pile and which are worthy of attentive pruning? If we don't have an angel of the Lord directing us to our mission field, how do we know when we are headed in the direction in which God wants us to go?

I confess that my deference for church polity might have left the Ethiopian eunuch dry on that desert road. I would have happily expounded upon the scripture, but I might have balked at presiding over an unauthorized sacrament. We have rules about such matters. The session must approve. Authorized representatives of the church must be present. Baptism is no private matter. Had the eunuch been properly instructed in the meaning and implications of baptism? Perhaps we could schedule a time to get together in a week and talk more about his request. Meanwhile, the fruit on the vine rots, and the branch begins to die.

How many times do we well-intended, committed church folk become barren branches in our earnest quest for decency and order? We put in place wedding policies, building use policies, funeral policies,

111

rules for who is eligible to be an official church leader, a check list for how to respond to someone seeking help, and on and on. We abide in our mostly well-meaning, thoroughly-vetted, liability-preventing policy manuals even as we look around and see that we are withering. We don't want to upset the status quo or ruffle the feathers of the faithful, even if it means dying on the vine.

The seeker, the one thirsty in the desert, asked us, "What is to prevent my being baptized?" And we get out the ever-expanding three-ring binder and say, "Well… first of all…"

Where are we abiding? Where do we live? What is nearest and dearest to our heart? Is it the historic communion ware or the Body of Christ? Is it the newly renovated fellowship hall or the men and women sleeping on the street? Is it the need to be right or Jesus' call to be merciful?

Branches that bear fruit are connected to the vine. They live inextricably with Jesus Christ. The litmus test they use to make decisions is not, "What's our liability?" but instead, "What does love call us to do?"

Such a calculation flies in the face of common sense, cultural norms, and prudent pragmatism. Asking the question "What does love require?" reveals answers that are always met with resistance, skepticism, and often disdain. And yet, living into those answers draws us close to Christ and enables us to abide in him no less than Jesus abides with the Father.

Living out the answers to the question "What does love require of us?" will inevitably bear good fruit, and yet will always involve pruning, sometimes radical and painful. That's the rub of this text from John. The branches that bear good fruit must endure change and loss. Abiding in Jesus never allows us to get too comfortable. Jesus gives the gift of peace, not worldly security and safety. Loving as Jesus calls us to love puts us on desert roads and other less than hospitable places.

One ruling elder I know exceeds in bearing good fruit. His joy in abiding in Jesus Christ draws others to him. His stalwart reliance on the grace and power of God is like a magnet that pulls the entire faith community closer to Jesus and subsequently more apt to risk loving in ways that demand sacrifice and change. The lens through which he sees the world is not a flippant, WWJD? The filter through which he sifts every decision is one of love. This doesn't mean the answer is always clear, and it certainly leaves room for debate and disagreement, for planning and thoughtful boundaries. But never can the body get away with using simply a policy, procedure, or precedent as the final word. His call to love as Jesus loves demands serious, honest inspection of the fruit. Will our action bring us closer to what Jesus commands or not? That is the question we need to ask ourselves and one another.

Over the past several weeks, I have been reading old editions of the "Presbyterian Outlook." I have been reading issues from the early 1940s. I came across a statement from the Presbyterian women of a southern state regarding the segregation of denominational conference centers. They wrote:

"After much prayer, quiet meditation and earnestly seeking His will, we are impelled to offer you our suggestions concerning the teaching of Negro women and young people in leadership training. It is our belief that separate and distinct places of meeting for each race would result in exactly the kind of Christian relationship and attitude that we feel is our responsibility."

They went on to acknowledge their responsibility "for giving Christ to our Negroes" and noted that separate training centers "would result in true Christian social justice and properly discourage secular social intermingling."

The statement never once mentions the gospel or Jesus. The last line read: "The report was submitted to the board meeting on October 28, 1943 and was approved." Did anyone ask as they deliberated: What does love require? Will this action put us closer to Christ or farther away? If we are unwilling to abide with one another, how can we possibly abide in Jesus, the true vine to which all our branches are connected?

Calling out people from years ago doesn't require much courage, however. Holding ourselves accountable here and now does. Knowing that abiding in Jesus Christ demands pruning for transformative growth to occur, if our actions keep us comfortable and safe, we can be sure our branches will, sooner or later, be barren and dead, useful only as fuel for the fire. Only in taking the risks that love demands will be bear good fruit.

Where are the places ripe for sharing the gospel? Anywhere we abide in Christ. How will we bear good fruit? By following Christ's commands. What is the greatest commandment? To love God and your neighbor. What is the new commandment Jesus gives his disciples? Love one another. Therefore, in all we do, we must ask ourselves and one another: What does love require? Further, what does loving like Jesus look like? Living out the answer to that question will not only fill us with joy, but bring joy to the world as well.

This week:

- If you are a gardener, what is the role of pruning in maintaining a healthy garden? Are there ways in which you think God is pruning you or your faith community?
- Recall a recent church meeting or discussion. What decisions were made? What questions were asked? What factored into the final decisions?
- Who are the seekers in your community? To what desert roads might God be sending you to share the good news?
- Are there things that just need to go on the burn pile for the vine to be healthy?
- What does it mean to abide in Jesus?
- Jesus says that he shares these things that his disciples might have his joy and that their joy might be full. When have you experienced this kind of joy?

## Sixth Sunday of Easter
Acts 10:44-48; 1 John 5:1-6; John 15:9-17

Could even the Gentiles be our friends?

Could they be friends for whom we are to lay down our lives? Friends we are to love like Jesus loves us? If the Holy Spirit pours over the Gentiles, does that not mean that God has chosen them, too? If God abides in them and we abide in God, doesn't that mean we can't escape being close to each other?

Jesus reminded his friends that he chose them, not the other way around. Therefore, those whom God has chosen become part of our circle of concern in ways we heretofore could not have imagined. Committee meetings, parties, worship, work, family dinners — everything just got a whole lot more complicated.

When our gatherings include people of different cultures, languages, and experiences, very little can be assumed. Have you found yourself in a context where everything was unfamiliar? The attentiveness and energy required exhausts and sometimes overwhelms all involved. I remember visiting my brother on the campus of Gallaudet University, a university designed for the deaf/hard of hearing individuals. I don't know American Sign Language. Nothing made sense to me. My brother translated for me, but still I knew I was missing a good deal of the conversations happening all around me. Aware of my deficit, he took pains to include me, as did his friends. Without their generosity and patience and everyone's extra effort, I would have been a complete outsider.

Often, when visiting church members in large, regional hospitals, I witnessed other visitors struggle to navigate the parking deck, the entrances, the hallways, the various waiting rooms. Which elevator leads to what building? How do you operate the phone on the wall outside the locked doors of the ICU? Could you give me directions to the cafeteria? Bewilderment layered over worry and sadness and stress. So much energy was exerted to complete basic tasks.

Equally as often, the person in the hospital bed wondered how to work the nurse call button or remote control to the television. A tray of food was left untouched because no one thought to move it close enough or unwrap the silverware for the patient. Medical personnel came and went, sometimes letting the patient know who they were and why they were there, other times barely acknowledging that there was an individual residing within the standard-issue gown. Seeing the patient as a person requires extra effort, time, and energy.

The word in this Acts text that lingers in my consciousness is "astounded." Acts 10:45 reads, "The circumcised believers who had come with Peter were astounded that the gift of the Holy Spirit had been poured out even on the Gentiles." The circumcised believers were amazed that God might gift the Gentiles with the Holy Spirit. But the gift was undeniable because the Gentiles were speaking in tongues and extolling God. It seems Jesus chose them too, and the circumcised believers' friend group just got a whole lot bigger, more interesting, and complicated. Intentional effort, extra energy, patience, and goodwill will be required by Jews and Gentiles alike.

The one who speaks a different language, the one fumbling to find their way out of the parking deck, the one in the hospital gown or lab coat, the one who eats pork and the one who doesn't, the one who shows up two hours late and the one who always brings extra guests, the one whose sensibilities about personal space are different than my own, the one whose politics and pronouncements make me cringe, the one who doesn't know "Amazing Grace" or Psalm 23, the one I thought beyond redemption — God chooses to incorporate them all into the vine and therefore makes them my friend. Astounding. Jesus said *without these friends my joy is incomplete. If I don't love these friends and am not willing to die for them, then my joy cannot be complete.*

Life just got a lot more complicated. I must now slow down, take notice, stop and abide, and they must do the same. We can't just do what we've always done. We can't presume we all know what's required or expected, hoped for or needed. Once the Holy Spirit gifts us with one another, we are called upon to accept, nurture, and cherish our new God-given friends. We must be good stewards of our holy friendship. And the only way to do so is to follow Jesus' commandment and love one another.

I am reading Sally Kohn's book, *The Opposite of Hate: A Field Guide to Repairing Our Humanity*. Kohn is a liberal commentator who often appears on Fox News. She writes about seeking to connect with people with whom she vehemently disagrees, some of whom have written hateful things to her online. She wrote, "I found my answer in my Aunt Lucy."

Her Aunt Lucy "lives in the middle of the country and is a conservative Republican. She also loves me, my partner, and our daughter and welcomes us with open arms at every family occasion we manage to attend. The few times we have cautiously talked politics, Aunt Lucy has been curious and kind. Aunt Lucy watches Fox News, and eventually it dawned on me that most Fox viewers are probably just like her — decent, curious about the news, intending to learn, and do something good with the information. I started to picture my Aunt Lucy when I would go on Fox…. It made it easier for me to think, talk and act from a place of kindness, not hate — not to essentialize the invisible people on the other side of those screens but instead imagine my Aunt Lucy, someone I love and respect."

God gifts even the Gentiles with the Holy Spirit. Astounding. Now we are friends. Baptized members of the same family. We have been given the gift of one another with that outpouring of the gift of the Holy Spirit. Life just got a lot more complicated — more interesting — richer, better — harder. Our circle of concern just exploded. Our joy won't be complete without one another. Loving one another brings us closer to Jesus Christ. Following Jesus, abiding in him, draws us closer to one another. To accept, nurture, steward, and cherish the gift of our friendship, we must slow down, take notice, and remember not to take anything for granted.

Don't assume to understand. Gently ask questions of one another. Be generous with honest answers. Plan the meetings, meals, and gatherings with care, intentionality, abounding in hospitality that demonstrates the desire for all to be heard, fed, and included. Look at each other, face to face. What do you see? Bewilderment? Pain? Weariness? Contentment? Happiness? When you hurt each other, which of course you will, forgive one another as God in Christ has forgiven you. When you struggle to imagine that God has chosen this particular person to be a part of the household of God, picture Aunt Lucy, someone you love and respect, and act accordingly. Remind yourself that Jesus' commandments are not burdensome, but light. Jesus revealed all we need to know and promises to give us whatever we need. Unless we love one another, our joy can't be complete. Astounding.

This week:

- Are there people you have a difficult time seeing as friends? Why? How can you begin to change your view of them?
- Is there an "Aunt Lucy" in your life? Someone you love and respect, but with whom you deeply disagree? How do you hold those two truths in tension?
- When have you had an experience of being an outsider? Were there people who helped you become part of the group? Have you ever been the one attempting to welcome a new person?
- What does it mean that Jesus calls us friends? What does it mean for us to call one another friends?
- Have you witnessed individuals or groups of people brought together by the Holy Spirit?
- When have you experienced an outpouring of the Holy Spirit? What happened? How did you know it was the Holy Spirit at work?

## Ascension of the Lord
### Acts 1:1-11; Ephesians 1:15-23; Luke 24:44-53

For forty days, the risen Christ appeared to many, alive and speaking about the kingdom of God. He told his followers that the promised power of God will be given to them, soon. They were, and would be, his witnesses. They looked skyward as he ascended, then were told to stop looking up and start moving out into the world. Jesus, resurrected and alive, opened his disciples' eyes to understand the scriptures. He reminded them of the promised power of God soon to come. They were, and would be, his witnesses. He led them as far as Bethany before He blessed them and ascended to heaven. They were left to worship him and get to work in the world.

The texts appointed for the ascension of the Lord tell the story of the risen Christ's assuring presence, God's promised equipping and the Spirit's certain empowered sending. We get in these texts a clear mandate, a divinely ordained purpose, renewed and deepened understanding of scripture and certain, more than adequate, heavenly power even as Jesus' earthly presence come to an end. The question for we contemporary disciples is whether or not we take up the mantle, trust the promise, and bear witness exactly where we are and to take his message to the ends of the earth to which we are sent.

The risen Christ taught, spoke, and demonstrated his resurrected state, but he took us only as far as Bethany and then expected us to go the rest of the way in faith. Jesus ascended and disciples got going. Christ ascended, and the church took on Jesus' work in the world. If ever we question, and we do, the importance or role of the church, ascension ought to give us pause, humble us, and cause us to listen again for the voice of God in Christ and through scriptures. We, who have witnessed the saving love of God and received the entire litany of gifts outlined in Ephesians chapter 1, we have work to do in spreading the good news to those who have yet to hear it or whose circumstances mute it. Paul's prayer for the church at Ephesus applies to us, too.

119

May God give us the spirit of wisdom and revelation. May the eyes of our hearts be enlightened. May we know the hope to which we have been called, the great power of those who believe, the death-defying power that raised Jesus from the dead. These are the gifts to which we have access through Christ. These are the gifts the church has received and must share in Jerusalem, Judea, Samaria and the ends of the Earth.

There is wisdom, revelation, enlightened hearts, hope, evil stomping, death defeating, and sin vanquishing power. There is power of God, the Holy Spirit, the knowledge of the Word, and the presence of Christ. These are the gifts God bestows upon his disciples and on Christ's body, the church. How, then, can we do anything other than worship and return to our daily lives with great joy?

Our world now, as always, is fascinated with death, relishes destruction, exploits the vulnerable, and too often believes there are no alternatives to cruelty and violence. We, who are witnesses to the ways of Jesus, know better. We know the depths of despair at the death of our Lord and the unspeakable joy of experiencing his resurrected presence. We know that with God all things are possible. We know that wisdom and hope, grace and love, mercy and reconciliation are not only possible, but through Jesus Christ, they are inevitable. When we mark Jesus' ascension on the liturgical calendar we are challenged to not keep this divinely revealed understanding to ourselves. We are challenged to worship and then get moving. We are called to shout for joy and then enter the places of unspeakable pain with the saving love of God. We are called to be witnesses to God's glory, creation's goodness, humanity's beauty, the church's hospitality, Christ's peace and the Spirit's power right where we are, in Jerusalem, and wherever people are dying to hear the gospel.

Remember how Jesus opened your mind and heart, and do not keep this God-given knowledge to yourself. The world is in need of it and our Lord commissions us to share it.

This week:

- What do you know of Jesus, really know, how did you come to know it and when and how have you shared this knowledge?
- In Acts, the disciples wanted to know when God would restore the kingdom of Israel. Jesus told them it is not for them to know this. What question(s) do you want to ask Jesus? What, do you imagine, is his answer?
- Where is your Jerusalem? Your Judea? Your Samaria? Your ends of the earth?
- When have you felt empowered to bear witness to Jesus Christ? What happened? What did you say? How was your testimony received?
- What is the role of the church in your community? In our larger culture? How has the church's role remained the same and how has it changed over time?
- Pray the prayer for your faith community that Paul prays for the church at Ephesus.

## Seventh Sunday of Easter
Acts 1:15-17, 21-26; 1 John 5:9-13; John 17:6-19

What happens next? The seventh Sunday of Easter is all about what happens after resurrection and after Jesus' ascension. The whirlwind of fear, grief, more fear, confusion, joy, and nascent understanding gives way to a new normal. Judas (that one destined to be lost or the one allotted his share in this ministry, depending how one wants to understand the betrayer's role) has gone on to what? Glory? Judgment? Both? He fully knew and was fully known, and I am hoping that with God's great mercy, even Judas was surprised by grace. The eleven felt compelled to be twelve again and the lot fell on Matthias. We hear nothing more of Joseph, called Barabbas but known as Justus. I suspect he is like so many other disciples through the ages: He kept doing the work, doing his best to follow Jesus, trying to make his Christianity matter in his life and in the life of the world until he, too, met God face to face.

The twelve, then eleven, now twelve again must get on with the business of following Christ now that the earthly, resurrected Jesus has returned to his Father. They, like us, must live into a new, uncharted normal of being faithful to the One who calls and sends, promises the Holy Spirit and grants us peace, even when we are not so sure of all of those things.

The season of testimony begins — for the eleven, for Matthias and for us. The time to testify to what we have seen and know has come. Are we ready to tell the truth, the whole truth, no matter the cost, circumstance, or reception?

That is what is at stake for disciples of Jesus Christ and that is why Jesus prayed fervently that we would stay the course. *Protect them, God*, he prayed. *Sanctify them, God. Send them, God.* This chapter in John's gospel is like overhearing a private and intimate conversation between Jesus and Abba. Reading the pleading of Jesus on behalf of his friends makes one want to both lean in and turn away. Should we be privy to such raw emotion and heartfelt requests? Jesus fulfilled his mission and now they must fulfill theirs. Like him, the world will reject and persecute them. Grace and mercy are hard sells in a world that glorifies greed and celebrates retribution. *Protect them, God. Sanctify them in the truth that is increasingly rejected, God.*

That was the new normal, for the twelve, and for disciples ever since. Testify to the truth no matter the cost, knowing that Jesus prays for us and God protects us. Such stalwart testimony even in the face of the world's skepticism, rejection, and persecution somehow completes the joy of those who keep at it.

The reality of joy does not necessarily come with the affirmation and accolades of culture, but instead through a commitment to Christ's truth, no matter how often experienced, still sounds suspect. Why else do we keep chasing after that which does not satisfy instead of following Jesus Christ?

Why do we believers so often capitulate to the world rather than live the words received from our Lord?

If living in the way, the truth, and the life was easy, Jesus would not have prayed so fervently for us on the cusp of the end of his earthly life. We forget that the door is narrow and that while Jesus' burden is light and his yoke is easy, bearing his cross would mean losing our lives.

But what does such a sanctified life look like? If we are not caring for the poor in Calcutta or part of the confessing church in Nazi Germany, how do we testify to the truth? Live the disciples' new normal in our own daily life? If we aren't being rejected and persecuted, are we being faithful?

James Cone spoke to a group gathered at Saint Mark Presbyterian Church in North Bethesda, Maryland. The *Outlook* partnered with National Capital Presbytery and Saint Mark Church to bring Cone to speak about his book, *The Cross and the Lynching Tree*. He lectured with power and passion. He didn't pull any punches. He said at one point, something along the lines of it was a miracle African Americans didn't hate white people. Even while people like me were eager to hear his prophetic word, we squirmed a little at the truth he spoke plainly. During the question-and-answer period, a white woman shared sincerely her agreement with his points and then said, "But what do we do?" Again, honest, heart-felt, but somehow communicating that perhaps the task was too hard, big and intractable. Cone paused and then said something that will not leave me: "You know what you need to do. The question is, are you willing to do it?" He went on to ask if she, and others, were willing to pay the price that it will require to bring about justice long denied.

Cone shared his testimony, testified to the truth and then asked us: Will you do the same, no matter the cost? Will you do the good you know or capitulate to the evil that comes so easily?

Having heard the truth and believed, will we do what the truth requires?

Too often we imagine that doing what we know needs to be done is too hard, impossible. Hence, Jesus' fervent and continuous prayer: Sanctify them in the truth. Protect them. Send them.

Our new normal of discipleship requires that we testify to the truth no matter the cost, whatever our context. We are called to pay attention to the nudges and shouts that say: You know what to do, now do it.

Testifying to the truth means going out into the world, being aware of our neighbors, engaging in what impacts our communities for good or for ill, speaking up, standing beside and answering "yes" to paying the price for doing what we know God is calling us to do.

What does that look like? For some, it is caring for the poorest of the poor in the streets of Calcutta. For others, it is sheltering a Jewish family in their attic. For others, it is making sure all their local schools are safe and resourced with supplies and trained, fairly-paid teachers. For some, it could be studying the history of the place where they live, looking at the zoning laws and showing up at the planning commission meeting. For others, it is taking in a foster child or working on prison reform or fighting against gerrymandering.

For each and every disciple of Jesus Christ, Matthias, and the one known as Justus, for Peter, Martha, Mary, and the countless ones whose names were never recorded but whose testimony to the truth spoken and lived made an impact, it means being sent, going out, loving the world

God so loves, doing what we know Jesus calls us to do, no matter the price.

Jesus, pray for us.

This week:

- When you look around your community, what needs to be done? Are you willing to pay the price to do it?
- Have you ever shared your testimony? How do we share our testimony to our belief in Jesus Christ in words and in deeds?
- What does it mean to be sanctified? Sanctified in the truth?
- When Jesus prayed that his followers be protected, what do we need protection from?
- When have you experienced joy as result of your life of faith? Do we connect joy with our daily discipleship?
- Use the verses from John 17 as you daily prayer this week. Pay attention to the verbs and be conscious of them as you go about your day.

## Day of Pentecost
Acts 2:1-21

Pentecost is revolutionary.

An inbreaking of the Holy Spirit means a great equalizing has happened. The world as we have known it has been turned upside down and inside out. Men and women, young and old, slave and free — the Spirit pours over all. The distinct languages and cultures of the whole world's peoples become the Word of the Lord. Direct communication of the divine deeds of power happens, no translation needed. Everyone is on a level playing field when it comes to the power and outpouring of the Holy Spirit. No wonder onlookers are amazed, perplexed, and judgmental.

Then, as now, human beings categorize and compartmentalize. Residents of Judea don't hang out with the Egyptians. They don't talk to each other, because they can't talk to each other. They literally and figuratively don't speak the same language. Just like the cafeteria in any middle school, everyone knows who sits at what table: like sit with like, and no one dares cross the metaphorical lines, invisible but as evident as the yellow ones on the highway. Wind and flames are noteworthy, but their disruption pales in comparison to the multitude of languages spoken by the disciples and the Holy Spirit given to everyone. The old human categories no longer apply to the new community formed through Jesus Christ and ushered in by the Holy Spirit. No wonder onlookers are amazed, perplexed, and judgmental.

Pentecost is revolutionary because the wind blows down barriers and the flames burn down walls between peoples separated by geography, culture, language, nation, class, race, and every other human-created category.

Just like the prophet proclaimed: Now everyone will prophesy in languages that others understand, in ways never before heard, to people long pushed to the margins. God's deeds of power and Jesus' saving works are for everyone, and nothing will stand in the way of the Spirit's revolutionary witness.

Pentecost is revolutionary, turning upside down and inside out every human-constructed category, divide and barrier to God's constituting one family. Distinct languages remain, but now we can speak to one another and understand. Nothing will separate us from the love of God through Christ Jesus our Lord, and through the gift of the Holy Spirit, nothing will separate us from one another, either.

And yet, here we are divided. The income gap grows, schools have re-segregated, most neighborhoods are homogeneous and churches — well, look around your sanctuary this Sunday. What happened to the revolution of Pentecost?

Like so many revolutions, the initial fervor and excitement gives way to a yearning for the familiar, even if the status quo was oppressive, limiting and less than life-giving. Better the constraining categories we know than doing the work of learning a whole new way of life.

The church traded the revolution of Pentecost for the comfort and complacency of silos of sameness. Pentecost has become the day on the liturgical calendar to celebrate the birthday of the church, instead of a day to remember that our entire world should be turned upside down and inside out when we commit to following Jesus Christ. Pentecost means that our circles of concern are expanded and multiplied. We are to be bilingual, trilingual, multilingual — always striving to speak more fluently and listen more closely until we come to a place where we know each other's languages so well that we dream one another's dreams.

What happened to the revolution of Pentecost? Where did the wind and flame of the Spirit go? When was the last time something in the church or in the community caused you to be utterly perplexed because you could never have imagined anything like it?

The Spirit continues to move, but too often we have heard the wind and barricaded ourselves in a windowless room until we are certain the gusts have moved past us. The Spirit blows where it wills, and if we run away when we hear the sound of it, it will blow elsewhere.

After revolution comes the hard, time-consuming, slow work of building a new order: a new way of life together. That's true for

Pentecost, too. A Spirit-constituted community, if it is to last and grow, requires work. Speaking another's language is challenging. Hearing someone speak a language they have not yet mastered calls for patience. The rubble of once formidable walls must be addressed, hauled away, recycled, reused. Creating a new common vocabulary comes only with time and shared experience. The pull of the old, familiar categories, patterns and our own native language is strong. No wonder we'd rather sing "happy birthday," blow out the candles, and go back to the same pew we've sat in for years. Spirit-community asks not just a lot from us, but everything we've got.

I had the profound gift of hearing Willie James Jennings of Yale lecture at Union Presbyterian Seminary. (Sprunt Lectures, May, 2018) In his last lecture he said this provocative statement: "Too many pastors have become the high priests of segregation." He went on to explain that they have "settled for love of their own people rather than using love to create a new people." Celebrating the birthday of the church on Pentecost is settling for love of our own people. Recognizing the barrier-breaking, new-community-constituting revolution and attempting to learn another's language — now that's stepping into the wind and flame of the Spirit and attempting to create a new people.

During the question-and-answer period, a person in the sanctuary asked how we pastors might move away from being high priests of segregation. Jennings replied, "I tell pastors: Think very carefully about your loves... make sure your life gives witness to a wider love." That's the power of Pentecost. The Spirit gives us the ability to imagine a wider love, beyond our own people, expanded into all of God's creation.

Every year when Pentecost rolls around on the liturgical calendar and we dust off the red stole, we are challenged to learn a language that is not our own, a language the Spirit will give us the ability to speak, a language that we will need to practice long after the visible, perplexing flames have left the room. Once God ushers in the revolution of the intimate, we are tasked with building a whole new life together, and that takes patience, intention, work, forgiveness, and grace.

Pentecost is far more than the church's birthday; it turns the whole world inside out and upside down. If we aren't perplexed, amazed, or confused at what's happening in our communities of faith, it may be time to blow out the candles and turn off the lights. It may be time to get out from behind our walls, meet the Cretans and Arabs, learn their languages, and expand our lives.

This week:

- Have you ever tried to learn another language? What did it feel like with you tried to speak in it? Were you understood?
- There are many other "languages" we need to speak if we are to share the good news of Jesus Christ in our contexts. Which one(s) are most pressing in yours? What do you need to learn about your community in order to understand and be understood?
- What do you find perplexing, confusing, amazing? Could it be that is a place or circumstance where the Holy Spirit is blowing?
- What are your loves? How do you need to widen them?
- Read Acts 2:1-21 out loud. What strikes you when you read it? Meditate on that part of the passage and note what you noticed as you pray.
- When have you had a revolutionary experience of the Holy Spirit?

Trinity Sunday
John 3:1-17


"Born OK the first time," the bumper sticker read.

Many who read it likely wondered what it meant. Of those who knew what it meant, many of those were likely offended. A small handful of people knew what it meant and chuckled. Born okay the first time, no need to be born again. All is well here. I admit to being in the third category of people named above. I knew what the bumper sticker meant and I chuckled. A Presbyterian growing up in the South, I'd run up against being asked, "Are you saved?" or "When were you saved?" multiple times. I'd even been asked if I had been born again. Nope. *Born OK the first time*. Saved a few thousand years ago with Jesus' death and resurrection. All is well. Nothing to see here. Thanks (no thanks) for asking.

I stand by my Presbyterian response to the "Are you saved?" question. I lean toward the Presbyterian Church (USA)'s Study Catechism's answer to question 38: "Will all human beings be saved? No one will be lost who can be saved. The limits to salvation, whatever they may be, are known only to God. Three truths above all are certain. God is a holy God who is not to be trifled with. No one will be saved except by grace alone. And no judge could possibly be more gracious than our Lord and Savior, Jesus Christ." I appreciate Calvin and predestination, painful as it is to read sentences like these: "We call 'predestination' God's eternal plan by which he has determined what he wanted to do with each person. For he did not create all in like condition, but he ordains some to eternal life, others to eternal damnation, so according to the end for which a person is created, we say that he is predestined to life or to death." (Institutes of the Christian Religion, 1541 French Edition)

Perhaps all is not well, but, clearly, the limits of salvation, whatever they are, are known only to God and determined solely by God. That's the gift, really, of our Reformed theology. Salvation is unearned, works of righteousness a foolish notion, our making a decision for Christ pure hubris. Jesus says, "I chose you, you did not choose me."

But here we have Nicodemus, a Pharisee, a leader of the Jews, seeking Jesus out in the night because he knew there was something powerful and important about this teacher, sent from God who performed remarkable signs. The descriptors of each character in this story are worth noting. A Pharisee named Nicodemus, a leader of the Jews who called Jesus by the title rabbi, one who had come from God, evident through his miraculous deeds. These descriptors are correct of each, but both lacking as well. Nicodemus could not fully see the kingdom of God, religious leader though he was, he mistook Jesus for an earthly rabbi rather than the Messiah, the Son of God, who was not just from God but of God. Nicodemus, Pharisee, leader of the Jews, was not yet a disciple of Jesus Christ because of his lack of vision, and his inability to call Jesus not just rabbi, but Lord. Born okay the first time, but blind from birth. Unable to see what was here. Unable to see who was there, right in front of him.

That's what was at stake in this exchange. Nicodemus lacked the vision to see that the kingdom of God had come to earth and was standing right in front of him. The ability to see precluded the confession of faith and that vision comes through submitting to the power of the Spirit and the water. The Spirit blows where it wills. The agency belongs to God, but let's give Nicodemus his due: He gave in to the promptings that brought him to Jesus that night, promptings that continued until we read of Nicodemus joining Joseph of Arimathea at the time of Jesus' burial. "Nicodemus, who had first come to Jesus by night, also came, bringing a mixture of myrrh and aloes, weighing about a hundred pounds. They took the body of Jesus and wrapped it with spices in linen cloths, a according to the burial customs of the Jews... and the tomb was nearby, they laid Jesus there" (John 19:39-42). Nicodemus, it would seem, has come to see Jesus differently than he did in the middle of the night. Nicodemus, Pharisee, leader of the Jews, follower of Jesus, his understanding of the rabbi so changed that his understanding of himself was transformed as a result, so radically new and different it might best be described as being born again.

The question is not "Are you saved?" but instead, "Do you see?" It's like those optical illusion drawings that contain an old couple and a young woman; even when we know both images are there, usually we can only recognize one or the other and willing ourselves to see the one we don't never works. Instead we must simply continue to look, be patient and open to the possibility that there is more than what we first observed and allow the image to appear as if from out of nowhere, always there, but only seen after opening ourselves to new undertanting can we see it.

Rabbi, teacher from God — Jesus — that's who and what we see in the dark of night. Those are powerful signs that get our attention and move us closer to the one performing them because we are curious and want to know more. That's all we know. We don't yet see him as the Son of Man, the Messiah, the Lord, our Lord. The winds of the Spirit have gotten us this far, but the water and the Spirit still need to work on us more. Jesus said we must be born again, and though we take that literally, we still don't understand. We wonder what in the world he was talking about. We leave confused by this rabbi, a teacher who should make things clearer, not muddy the waters. We believe that we are born okay the first time, after all.

Yet we can't stop thinking about Jesus' words, the signs, or the power of his presence. Something even emboldens us to speak up to those in our own circles on behalf of Jesus. Nicodemus, a Pharisee, a leader of the Jews, said to the chief priests and other Pharisees who wanted the temple police to arrest Jesus, "Wait a minute, that's not how our laws work." Nicodemus saw that justice was being perverted by his tribe and he did one of the most difficult things there was to do: He stood up to his own friends, leaders, and colleagues. He stood up for the very one they want to condemn. He said, "Our law does not judge people without first giving them a hearing to find out what they are doing, does it?" To which his fellow Pharisees responded: "Surely you are not also from Galilee, are you? Search and you will see that no prophet is to arise from Galilee."

Nicodemus did search and what he saw, what he was beginning

to see, might be so radically different than what he expected, what he previously thought he knew, it could be characterized as a new birth.

The question for us on this Trinity Sunday is not "Are you saved?", but rather "Do you see?" What we see will be revealed, if we have indeed been born again, and shown in how we describe Jesus, and therefore how we understand others, making our new vision known to them. Rabbi, teacher from God, Son of God, Messiah, Lord of all, my Lord and Savior, the one for whom I will stand even at the risk of losing my closest allies and friends, even at the risk of my own life because I am not only or primarily a religious leader, but a follower of Jesus Christ. *Born OK the first time*, but through the water and the Spirit born again, now able to see the kingdom of God right in front of me, all around us, never absent from us. Everything to see, here.

This week:

- Have you ever been asked if you were born again or when were you saved? How did you respond? What is the value of thinking of salvation as incumbent upon our making a conscious decision to follow Jesus? What is the theological danger in that approach?

- In our Reformed understanding that salvation is through grace alone and faith alone, do we risk losing accountability for our actions and the way we live? If there are risks to understanding "personal salvation" as reliant on our making a choice, what are the theological hazards of election and predestination?

- How does your faith in Jesus Christ make a difference in your daily living? Is it evident that you have been born by water and the Spirit?

- Have you experienced a radical experience of "new seeing?" A conversion experience? What happened? How did your life change as a result?

- Nicodemus is named three times in John's gospel: the text appointed for Trinity Sunday, again in chapter 7:50-51 and finally in chapter 19:39-42. Read each of these passages.

What do you make of these descriptions of Nicodemus? Do you see a progression in his understanding of who Jesus is? How has your understanding of Jesus evolved throughout your faith journey?

- How does this text from John inform your understanding of the Trinity?

1 Samuel 8:4-11; 2 Corinthians 4:13-5:1; Mark 3:20-35

Jesus had it coming at him from all sides. and we're only in the third chapter of Mark. Not only are the religious elites saying he is possessed by Satan, his own family thinks he is out of his mind. I wonder what the just appointed twelve think of this scene. The crowd is so boisterous, big, and needy that eating in Jesus' own home wasn't an option. Jesus' family sought to restrain him. The scribes say Jesus was ruled by the ruler of the demons. Jesus then called "them" and spoke to "them" in parables. Who, exactly, was "them"? The twelve? Jesus' family? The scribes? The crowds? All of "them?" Regardless, he launched into a lecture about Satan, a house divided, and tying up the strong man when breaking into a house. Oh, and then that bit about all sins being forgivable, except for blasphemy against the Holy Spirit (whatever that meant).

But wait, there's more! Jesus then was told that his family was outside asking for him, to which he replied: "Here are my mother and brothers! Whoever does the will of God is my brother and sister and mother."

Got all that?

What's going on in this text, plunked in between the appointment of the twelve and the blessedly familiar parable of the sower?

In short, a lot. This complex story with a story in the middle reveals a great deal about who Jesus is and what he came to earth to do. Jesus' declaration about who's kin to him and the binding of the strong man made it explicit that he had come to bring about a whole new order of connection, loyalty, and power. Jesus' mission was subversive, unexpected as a thief in the night, total and unstoppable. The established rules for who was in and who was out did not apply any more. Jesus came to bind up the forces of evil and take over the house and all who are within it. Those who joined him in fulfilling this divine mission — they were and are his family. Those who didn't? Well, they remained outsiders, looking in.

This story is offensive. Jesus rebuffed his family, thumbed his nose at those in religious leadership, and even compared himself to one who had broken into someone's home, tying up the owner and stealing from them. I suspect if I'd been there, I would have thought Jesus out of his mind, too. If I'd been Mary, I would have worried not only for my son's safety, but for mine and the rest of my family's. If I'd been Jesus' brother I would have done just about anything to stop the public embarrassment and danger Jesus was subjecting upon the family. Even now, I don't like Jesus to make me too conspicuous or put me too much at odds with the respected, revered, leaders of the day. I am happy to go to worship on Sunday and even read my Bible on the airplane, but I don't want anyone to think me as one of those "crazy Christians." I have been careful to couch my responses to questions, my comments on issues, and my selection of phrases to make sure that my faith is evident, but also rational, measured, and within socially acceptable parameters.

In short, I don't want Jesus' teachngs to cause offense, but that's exactly what he does in Mark's Gospel this week. He offends those closest to him, those with the greatest power to hurt him and even, I suspect, some in the crowd and the newly appointed apostles, too. Jesus offends because he upends everything we've heretofore thought sacred: family, religion, civility, established order, home, church, and country. Jesus calls us to give up all the loyalties that, in comparison to God, should be penultimate, but in practice become working idols that drive our decisions, thoughts and actions.

Therein lies the blasphemy against the Holy Spirit. Ched Myers in "Binding the Strong Man: A Political Reading of Mark's Story of Jesus," quoting Juan Luis Segundo noted: "What is not pardonable is using theology to turn real human liberation into something odious. The real sin against the Holy Spirit is refusing to recognize, with 'theological' joy, some concrete liberation that was taking place before one's very eyes." In other words, when we clean up Jesus to the point that his mission was no longer disruptive and offensive, we commit the unforgivable sin. We render Jesus so innocuous that instead of binding up the strong man and freeing the captives, we use him to bolster the status quo when it best benefits us. We conflate our wants, biases, and beliefs with Jesus' Words and mission — and that is blasphemy against the Holy Spirit.

This sin against the Spirit is pervasive and not the exclusive purview of any branch of the vine. We all use Jesus to support our own claims,we cherry-pick scripture. We completely ignore parts of the Bible and rationalize our behavior with other parts of scripture. We witness divine liberation, and label it demonic possession. We confuse the work of the devil with the mission of the Messiah and vice versa. Time and time again, we can see the speck in another's eye while failing to notice the log in our own. We say we want to quiet Jesus for his own good, when really it is our own reputation that we are concerned for. We make Jesus in our own image, instead of making sure we resemble his. We pretend that Jesus is polite, rather than disruptive.

Jesus is offensive. He came to make clear that our loyalty to God should trump all other loyalties, including those we've long held sacred. Jesus is offensive. He told the nice, respected, revered religious leaders they were not only misguided, they were instruments of evil. Jesus is offensive. He came like a thief in the night to upend the rule of those long in power. Jesus is offensive. He got close to crowds, called tax collectors, touched the unclean, and ate with sinners. Jesus is offensive. He spoke the truth to those in power, to us, to all. Jesus is offensive because he refused to go along with the practices of others, to bow down to long-accepted norms, to allow cultural or familial expectations to thwart his mission of binding up the brokenhearted and liberating those long held captive.

What was going on in this story of family conflict, needy crowds, conspiring scribes, newbie disciples, and Beelzebub? Nothing less than the overthrowing of an old, evil, oppressive order and Jesus' ushering in of God's divine one. What did Jesus' mother and brothers, binding up the strong man, a house divided, and blasphemy against the Holy Spirit have in common? They all show where we stand: on the side of Jesus' vision and mission of liberation, or Satan's side of oppression. They all reveal if we are part of Jesus' family — or not.

## Lectionary Reflections

This week:

- What is your gut reaction to this story from Mark? Why?
- In the text just prior to the one for this Sunday, Jesus appointed the twelve. They would be with Jesus, then go out and proclaim the message and "have authority to cast out demons." What does it mean to have this authority? Do Jesus' disciples today have this power? How does the reading for today inform your understanding of what it means to cast out demons?
- Look at other passages where the word "bind" or "binding" is used in Mark (Mark 5:3, 6:17, 15:1, 15:7). How is the word used in those passages? Any similarities between these passages?
- How do we make Jesus less offensive? Or do we? Do we, like Jesus' family, ever want to get Jesus to quiet down and stop drawing attention to himself and us?
- How do you understand "blasphemy against the Holy Spirit"? Why is this unforgivable?
- Do you think of Jesus' mission as subversive like someone breaking into another's home? Where else do you read of Jesus coming like a thief in the night?

## Proper 6/Ordinary Time 11

1 Samuel 15:34-16:13; 2 Corinthians 5:6-10 (11-13) 14-17;
Mark 4:26-34

I refuse to live like a character in a dystopian novel.

More and more, I hear sentiments of defeat, cynicism, and hopelessness. I understand such expressions of fear, grief, and frustration. Each day brings with it grim news of exploitation, suffering, and injustice. Each day dawns and still disease destroys, children bear burdens not of their own making, and human beings destroy one another as well as creation itself. It takes little effort to look around, shrug our shoulders, and say, "We're doomed."

We're doomed, and there is nothing we can do about it, so why bother getting engaged, giving resources, or working for change? Let's hunker down, keep our heads down, and try to avoid as much of the mess as we can. Or, let's protect what we deem as ours at all costs. Who can blame us? It's a dog-eat-dog world, as the saying goes.

I look at the news, read the paper, see images of children in cages, hear a translator on the radio echo the small voice of a child, telling of being given a teddy bear after being taken from her mother after they crossed our country's southern border and wonder: What kind of people have we become? The little girl says she used the teddy bear to wipe her tears. I cannot hold back my own as I listen.

I overheard a conversation in the gym locker room between two women talking about the "karma" that swept an elderly couple away in recent floods, killing them both. One said, "No one ever liked them." The other apparently had cared for the couple's animals and said, "Maybe they left me something!" They both cackled with laughter. I think: What kind of people have we become? We are doomed. I am living in a dystopian novel.

But these texts for this Sunday say that God does not see as we do. They say that God looks upon the heart, not outward appearances. The texts say: We walk by faith and not by sight. The texts say: We are always confident. The texts say: The love of Christ urges us on. We don't live to ourselves. We regard no one from a human point of view. Anyone who is in Christ is a new creation. The texts say: That the kingdom of God is like a mustard seed, tiny, insignificant, vulnerable, useless from all outward appearances, but explosive with potential and the promise to nurture, shade, hide, protect, give respite to all the nations, every bird of the air and the beasts of the land, too.

I refuse to live as if I am a character in a dystopian novel. I won't give up that easily. These texts won't let me. There is a miniscule mustard seed of faith that won't die, that keeps sprouting through the cracks of my hard-heartedness, fatigue, and cynicism. The story of which you and I, and all of us who claim to follow Jesus Christ — our story — is not one of fighting to the death, but fighting for life, abundant, beautiful, explosively, and insidiously good.

The verses in 2 Corinthians that come just after the ones appointed for this Sunday tell us: We have been given the ministry of reconciliation. We are ambassadors for Christ. We are chosen by God to lead, not because we look good or are good, but because God is good. We are small kingdom seeds that easily get trampled, eaten, washed away, or overtaken by weeds, but seeds that God will nonetheless bring to bud and flower, to expansive, irrepressible growth.

The story of which I am a part is a tall tale, of magical trees, that grant shade and shelter, food, and respite. The story I am going to tell is one of a mustard seed kingdom, where the last will be first and the first will be last, but thanks to the grace of God, everyone gets a seat at the table. I am going to tell the story of the texts for this Sunday, this day of resurrection, this eighth day of creation: New life is surely coming, we see with the eyes of God and what we see is beautiful, true, just, lovely, kind, grace-filled, and so glorious in its flora and fauna that you are going to look up, look out, and burst into tears for the shear goodness of it all and God will wipe every tear from your eyes, not with a teddy bear, but with the very hand of the most high.

I refuse to live as if I am a doomed character in a dystopian novel, determined to do whatever it takes to survive, the rest of the world be damned. We walk by faith and not by sight. We live not for ourselves, but for the sake of Jesus Christ. The love of Christ urges us on and we regard no one from a human point of view, but see each and every one as made in God's image, called good and beloved.

I attended a panel discussion on immigration this week. The panel included three lawyers, an activist, and a poet. They were joy-filled, not optimistic, often discouraged, but ever hopeful. The poet, Seth Michelson, has worked with youth in one of two of our nation's maximum-security detention centers, where some of the unaccompanied minors who have crossed the border are held. These children have been through hell, having witnessed or been forced to participate in horrendous violence. The detention facility in which they are held is being sued due to the horrendous conditions within it. However, these children are still suffering.

Seth Michelson edited a book of poetry written by these kids, *Dreaming America: Voices of Undocumented Youth in Maximum-Security Detention*. Of all the panelists, the poet relentlessly urged those of us in attendance not to give into the narrative of hopelessness.

He read some of the poems from the book. The poems have no name attached, because revealing the identity of the author was forbidden. He read poems that expressed dreams, hopes, loss, and beauty. Most of the youth are illiterate. They are not guaranteed legal representation. They have no idea when they will be released, or where they will go once they are. Some, so despondent, have taken to cutting themselves and banging their heads against the walls and floor. And yet, as the poet said, even here there is beauty, goodness, and hope.

One of his young poets wrote from detention of his hopes to create homes for those without them and safe space for the animals as well.

I hope to do that, too. I refuse to live as if I am a character in a dystopian novel. I am going to lead a mustard seed life until all the birds of the air have a place to make a nest, every single nation supports the poor and hunger is no more and there is a great, beautiful, shaded, lovely place for all to live, the animals, too. That's the story of which I want to be a part.

## Lectionary Reflections

This week:

- What are the narratives you hear? How are they like or unlike the narrative of the gospel?
- How do we regard no one from a human point of view? How do we walk by faith and not by sight?
- Notice beauty and signs of hope. Pause to give thanks for them.
- Why does Jesus talk and teach in parables? Are there ways we could do likewise?
- When have you been surprised by someone or something and realized that there was more than what you initially saw, thought or assumed?
- What is the narrative you are living and how is that story evident in your daily living?

# Proper 7/Ordinary Time 12
1 Samuel 17:1a-49; Mark 4:35-41

Power is the *topic du jour* this Sunday: Who's got it? When do they use it? What does it reveal about the one who wields it? Where is it evident? How do people respond to it?

Let's start with 1 Samuel: In this iconic tale of the winning underdog, who has the power?

All evidence suggests that Goliath and his crew of uncircumcised Philistines have the power. They have the size and strength to defeat those of their choosing. Goliath has the power and he enjoys it, taunts those without it and engenders fear in all around him. He exercises his power at will and without mercy as one after another falls victim to his violence. Who's got the power? The physically strong and well-armed, they've got the power.

I am thinking you can come up with a Goliath-like list to hold up as "exhibit A" this Sunday. Who's got the power? Military regimes have the power. Human traffickers have the power. Coyotes have the power. Abusers have the power. Who's got the power? Goliath has the power! Always has, always will! Watch the History Channel, read the newspaper, tune in to the 24-hour news cycle, Goliath has the power!

But what about that David upstart? The one who annoyed the fire out of his bigger, older brothers? Who did he think he was? Shouldn't he have been tending the sheep? What business did he have on the battlefield? How could he possibly have had any power?

In good biblical fashion, there is a role reversal and the shepherd boy has come with just the right skills and tools at just the right time. Bears and lions aren't so different from bullies. Smooth stones, well timed and well-thrown, can take out even a giant. David had power, too, and he was confident in it and unafraid — that's the key. Goliath has counted on everyone being terrified in the face of his might, but not David. David knew he, too, has power, and the source of his power cannot be defeated. That's the real difference. David knew the true source of power and it was the God of Israel who demanded justice, upheld the weak, and refused to abandon the vulnerable.

David knew he couldn't lose. The victory was as sure as won, so he entered the battle — not with Saul's armor — but with the tools and skills he knew, the ones God had given to him to use for God's purposes and for God's glory.

Who has the power? God has the power and those who trust in that source and seek that one's glory may not be invincible, but their cause is unstoppable.

Where are the examples of God's power? Where do you look to hold up "exhibit B" to your people? Le Chambon-Sur-Lignon? Selma? South Africa? A teenage girl on an Afghanistan school bus? Examples are all over scripture, of course. Joseph, Rahab, Daniel, Shadrach, Meshach, and Abednego, plus the woman at the well and the women at the tomb... all examples of God's strength in weakness. Share the power of God with your people through a few of these stories, and you provide some biblical education that is far from boring. But don't stop there, because surely God is still at work in your community. Who do you know who is bold like David? Fearless in their faith in God? Relentless in standing up to the bullies of our day?

If you have not read Timothy Tyson's *Blood Done Sign My Name* get a copy and start reading. If you are like me, it will put what you fear in your ministry into perspective and might bolster your courage and cause you to break out your prophetic voice with a little more frequency. Read about Miss Amy in chapter four and consider the Miss Amys that you know. Jonothan Kozol's *Ordinary Resurrections* is full of people powerful only through faith and the bold use of seemingly paltry gifts. You see, there are Davids facing off Goliaths all the time. This week pay attention, and you will see them too.

Keep in the front of your consciousness those who, what, where, when, and how questions regarding power and I suspect you will have too much material for one sermon. Make note of the Goliaths — they are everywhere — but be ever mindful of the David's God is calling to stand up to them. (Who knows? It could be you and your congregation.)

Who has the power? In Mark's gospel it is all God, all the time, over all that threatens to undo us. It is both immediate and cosmic. Jesus healed the sick and calmed the storm. Demons knew who he was, yet his closest followers did not. Although the disciples knew he could do something, they weren't so sure he would. Parents brought their children to Jesus, while religious leaders plotted to kill him. Power, power, who has the power?

These few verses from Mark make it abundantly clear that God has the power. Jesus has the power. Even the wind and sea obeyed him. Mark's hearers would have heard echoes of Psalm 107 (check out verses 25-32) and Psalm 65. I suspect they would have recalled the exodus, too, what with the parting of the Red Sea and all. No wonder there was fear or awe or some combination thereof on the part of the disciples. This "Peace, be still!" moment reveals not just the what and when and how and where of power, it reveals the *who*. They may be asking the question, but the fact that the disciples are voicing it implies that they, on some level, know the answer. The living God is in the boat with us, now what do we do?

That's the next question: If the living God is in the boat with us, not an arm's length away every moment, what do we do now? If God and God's power is for us, who can be against us? And what does that mean for our living?

Daniel Mendelsohn, in his book about family members killed in the Holocaust titled *The Lost: A Search for Six of Six Million*, wrote this: "The Holocaust is so big, the scale of it is so gigantic, so enormous, that it becomes easy to think of it as something mechanical. Anonymous. But everything that happened, happened because someone made a decision. To pull a trigger, to flip a switch, to close a cattle car door, to hide, to betray."

Goliath was so big, the scale of that power and evil so gigantic, so enormous. It became easy to think he was inevitable, undefeatable, maybe even eternal. But every day we have choices that reveal who we believe has the power. We can choose to give into Goliath, or we can choose to remember that God and God's power are in the boat with us, regardless of the size or threat of the storm. Our actions reveal to whom we've given the power in our lives.

Who has the power? The one who even the wind and sea obey, the one who does indeed care if we are perishing, the One who gifts us with a spirit not of cowardice, but rather a spirit of power, love, and self-discipline (2 Timothy 1:7 NRSV). Use the experience, the skills, and the tools God has given you, and preach knowing that you have the power of God not only in the boat with you, but in your every breath.

This week:

- Read the epistle lesson for this week: (2 Corinthians 6:1-13). Consider what these verses have to say about power and strength.
- Read the daily headlines either in print or online. Who are the Goliaths? Do you notice any Davids standing up to them?
- Read Mark 4:35-41 pausing to consider each verse. Since this is a short passage, take the time to read/pray it *lectio divina* style.
- Consider the disciples' reaction to the storm in Mark 4. They seemingly trusted Jesus could do something, but they appeared uncertain that he would do something. Have you ever felt this way? When? What happened? Where are other biblical passages where Jesus' care was questioned? (Hint: The same word is used in Luke 10:40.)
- Another prominent theme in both the 1 Samuel text and the one from Mark this week is fear. How do we keep our fear at bay? Of what are we most afraid? Do a brief word study of "fear" and note the details of those passages. Be sure and include the words of assurance that are often part of those texts.
- Consider the quote from Daniel Mendelsohn's book, "But everything that happened, happened because someone made a decision." Do you agree? Theologically, what does that say about our agency and God's? Be mindful of the decisions

146

you make this week. What do they reveal about where you put your trust? Do they show a spirit of cowardice or of power, love and self-discipline?

## Proper 8/ Ordinary Time 13
2 Samuel 1:1, 17-27; 2 Corinthians 8:7-15; Mark 5:21-43

Notice first, the expansive scope of Jesus' circle of concern. The crowd pressed him. The crowd pressed and followed him. Religious leaders begged for his help. A vulnerable, socially isolated woman did not go unnoticed by him. A young girl would not be left for dead. Jesus revealed in the fast-paced, action-packed story that his care and compassion encompassed everyone. If we get nothing else from this text this week, this lesson would go a long way in our own vision of the church's mission. No one should be beyond the circle of our concern or care. In fact, many people, separated by human boundaries are so often written off, labeled as too far gone, shunned and judged, are the very ones the church ought to be noticing, hearing, seeing, touching, and helping to heal.

Spend some time pondering this truth and then do an inventory — a mental one or an physical one, of who attends your house of worship and who does not. Why? Take note of where energy, resources, and attention are spent in your outreach ministry. Do a quick review of the budget; the church's and perhaps your personal one, too. Who is touched by these aspects of our corporate life, by us, and who is left to suffer on the margins? Perhaps an exercise of discernment would be in order as a result of these observations. Despite the crowds, the multitude of needs, the chaos, and size of the throng, Jesus responded to all people with specific needs, not at the expense of the others, but in sequential, focused attention. Would that model be one we could, on our own scale, emulate?

Notice, secondly, the diverse way people found and continue to find their way to Jesus. Jairus, a man of status and power, came to Jesus head on. He barreled forward. I imagine him pushing himself through the crowd, his daughter's life hanging in the balance as he told Jesus directly what he wanted. Heal my daughter, he begged, humbling himself, and falling at Jesus' feet. And Jesus responded. The woman, on the other hand, aware she was not supposed to be in such proximity to Jesus, clear she was unclean, snuck through the crowd, trying to remain unseen. She made a mad grab at the back of Jesus' garment, her hope or desperation so great, she lunged at whatever aspect of Jesus she could reach. Jesus responded.

Jesus knows our seeking of him, even when we fear to make that longing evident to others or even to our Lord. Jesus met both Jairus and the long-suffering woman as they were, however they came to him, with compassion, attention, and care. But there is one more person to whom Jesus' responded in this story: Jairus' daughter, and she had no agency at all. She did not come to Jesus, Jesus came to her by way of her loving father. When we do not have the ability to seek Jesus out ourselves, when we are utterly incapacitated, Jesus comes to us. Jesus takes seriously our intercessions and interventions on behalf of others. A group of people made a hole in the roof through which to lowered down their paralyzed friend, and Jesus responded. Parents brought their little children to Jesus and he blessed them. Jairus pleaded on behalf of his daughter and Jesus heard his heart's desire, dropped everything, and went.

Jesus' circle of concern is ever-expanding. We participate in that growth when we come to him for the sake of another. This reality might inform our prayer life, color our holy imagination, and propel us to act. Jesus responds to us, however we make our way to him and Jesus comes to us when we cannot possibly make our way to him. And yet, in this story, we cannot forget that there were, and will always be, those who mock the life-giving power of the Son of God. Always, always, there will be some who say, "It will never work." Always, always, there will be some who refuse to believe that transformation is possible. Always, always, there will be some who think that there are specific human beings not worthy or God's time and attention or subsequently, ours. Why waste your time? They will ask. Why waste our resources? They will argue. Do a cost benefit analysis and make better investments, exert your energy where there will be a better return, there are other needs more readily met, so move on.

## Lectionary Reflections

This story, however, revealed Jesus' unwillingness to write off any one of God's beloved children. Powerful leaders, vulnerable people, powerless children, all of them belong to God, none of them will be forgotten, Jesus came to save them all. The question for us as we read this story is: where are we in it? That, no doubt, changes over time, and perhaps remembering when we have been Jairus, or the long-suffering woman, or the incapacitated little girl, will keep us from laughing at Jesus' compassion and instead extend it in our ever expanding circles.

This week:

- How have you made your way to Jesus? How did Jesus respond to you?
- When have you interceded on behalf of another?
- Are there times when you have been tempted, or given into the temptation, to write someone off as too far gone and unworthy of help or unable to receive it?
- How do we keep from giving into despair or being overwhelmed with the needs of the world?
- How big is your circle of concern? Are there ways God is calling you to expand it?
- How do we discern how best to help others? Are they ways of helping that actually hurt?

## Proper 9/ Ordinary Time 14
2 Samuel 5:1-5, 17-27; 2 Corinthians 12:2-10; Mark 6:1-13

Jesus' instructions to his disciples in Mark's gospel remind me of a packing list for camp.

Campers should bring: flashlight, sunscreen, bug spray, toothbrush, rain poncho, flip flops, tennis shoes, swimsuit, enough shorts and T-shirts for a week, towels, and toiletries. Be sure to pack a jacket or sweatshirt, as it may get cold in the evenings. What to leave at home: cell phone, electronics, pocketknives, and money. Items to be sure to bring and those to be sure to leave indicate the nature of the activities and the kind of community that will define camp. Practicality wins the day, with comfortable, weather-appropriate clothing that allows the wearer to move freely without worrying about getting dirty. Cell phones, computers, and the like are prohibited: they are too distracting. Campers must be able to focus on the tasks and people at hand. Money isn't necessary, serving as a hindrance to keep track of rather than a means to acquire goods. Everything else that the campers need will be provided. The first step to a positive camp experience, to learning and growing, to making friends and gaining skills, is packing correctly. No one wants to be caught in the deluge of an afternoon thunderstorm without a poncho or to end up deep in the woods minus bus spray.

Following the instructions on the packing list allows for full participation in the experience to come. This is true for summer campers, and this is true for disciples of Christ. If those of us who follow Jesus are to engage totally in the work to which we've been called, we first need to get the packing list right and Jesus said: pack light.

Jesus said his burden was light, and yet we often load ourselves up with superfluous stuff. Jesus told the twelve to take only a staff, no bread, no bag, no money. Wear sandals, put on two tunics. Go in pairs. Now, get moving. Notice that these items allowed for mobility and flexibility. The disciples weren't taking time every morning to re-pack the donkey. Nor were they dragging a roller bag behind them, stopping every few feet to adjust their shoulder bag or rebalance boxes or backpacks. The packing list indicated that they were expected to be on the move, never to get too comfortable in one place, and not to be on the lookout for the nicest home, but content with whatever accommodations were offered.

The lack of baggage carried by Jesus' followers extended to metaphorical baggage, too. "Shake the dust off your feet." Keep moving, mentally, spiritually. Don't obsess over those who won't hear you or those who dismiss you or those who ridicule you. Did you pay attention to what happened to Jesus in his hometown? There are people who, even with Jesus himself right in front of them, refuse to believe the word or see the work of God. If folks don't recognize and value Jesus, inevitably many will fail to welcome those who come in Jesus' name. Let it go. Keep moving. Keep preaching, teaching, anointing, healing, and confronting evil. Don't worry about the outcome. Don't carry grudges. Let go of any need for retribution. Don't give into anger, fear, disillusion. As it turns out, not being weighed down by this kind of baggage can prove much harder than leaving even our cell phones behind.

On weeks (months, years) when every news report details violence, exclusion, a trampling of the weak, exploitation of the vulnerable, or suffering upon suffering, shaking the dust off our feet seems almost impossible. Preaching, teaching, healing, anointing, confronting evil, casting out demons — what's the use? Does our ministry make a difference? Does our witness matter? Not many people are opening their doors and inviting us in. We're hitting wall after wall, real or proposed. Our sandals are worn, our tunics stained, our feet, bodies, minds, and spirits are weary. Maybe it would be best to give it up and go back home. Perhaps we should feign illness so that the camp nurse calls our parents to come and fetch us. Maybe we should bury ourselves in the distractions of cell phones, laptops, like-minded Twitter rants and feel-good cat videos on Facebook. Forget shaking off the dust. How about a nice, hot shower that washes it down the drain, and lets us be free of it forever?

Packing light may well be difficult, but letting go of the baggage of cynicism, contempt, anger, fear, and just plain fatigue is harder. And yet that is what Jesus instructs us to do. Disciples are not greater than their masters. Jesus was rejected, questioned, judged and persecuted. He did what he could in his hometown and when he could do no more, he went into other towns. He kept moving. Kept proclaiming. Kept healing, casting out demons, confronting evil, calling out oppressors and alleviating suffering. The affirmation or acceptance of others was not a prerequisite for his ministry, and it cannot be for ours either. When tangible results are elusive, we trust that God gives the growth, sometimes underground and unseen, to those of us throwing the seed.

Civil rights leader John Lewis, on a week when it would be all too easy to give into helplessness and hopelessness, tweeted the following: "Do not get lost in a sea of despair. Be hopeful, be optimistic. Our struggle is not the struggle of a day, a week, a month, or a year, it is the struggle of a lifetime. Never, ever be afraid to make some noise and get in good trouble, necessary trouble. #goodtrouble"

Shake off the dust and keep moving. Don't get bogged down in the baggage of despair. We don't follow Jesus for a day or a week, but for a lifetime. We are disciples of Jesus Christ, who went all the way to the cross to redeem the world, including those who rejected him, tortured him and killed him on Good Friday.

Like the first twelve, Jesus gives us instructions, a packing list, and even more, a new commandment: love one another. Keep moving, preaching, praying, healing, anointing, casting out demons, confronting evil, alleviating suffering, and bringing good news to the poor. Go together. Rest in those places and with those people who welcome you. Notice the beauty and good trouble along the journey. Don't forget that the grace of your baptism is sufficient for your calling, because it is God's grace, so sufficient, in fact, that you don't need to haul any baggage, literal or metaphorical. Grab your staff, find a fellow disciple, and go out into the world to show the love of Jesus Christ. Let those with ears to hear, listen, and those who can't, well, shake off the dust and keep going.

This week:

- What baggage do you need to leave behind to go where Jesus sends you?

- What's the significance of having the story of Jesus' rejection by his hometown just before he sent out the twelve disciples? Note that the death of John the Baptist came right after the sending of the twelve. How does that inform your reading of this Sunday's text?

- Is there a contemporary way to say, "Shake the dust off your feet?" What about the last part of that instruction, "as a testimony against them?" How is shaking off the dust a testimony?

- Jesus gave his disciples "authority over unclean spirits." What does this mean? Do we have this authority? If so, what form does that authority take in our discipleship?

- How are we following Jesus' instructions? If we are being sent out, where and to whom are we going?

- Have you ever felt as if your ministry, your life of faith, has not made a difference or had an impact? How did you "shake off the dust" and keep at it?

## Proper 10/ Ordinary Time 15
## 2 Samuel 6:1-5, 12b-19; Mark 6:14-29

For a gospel into that whole brevity thing, Mark devoted a lot of space to the account of John the Baptist's death.

There is no birth narrative in Mark. Mark began with (wait for it...) John the Baptist. Jesus' baptism and temptation are allotted five verses total. The account of Jesus' rejection in Mark's gospel leaves out copious details found in Luke. We don't even get the story of the resurrection in Mark's compact recording of the life and death of Jesus. And yet, the writer of Mark gives a sixteen-verse rendering of John the Baptist's beheading by Herod. What was so important to Mark in this gruesome story in which there were no good actors, save the one whose head ended up on a platter?

I don't think this is a mere morality tale about power and its abuse, although that's in there. Nor do I think Mark relished the horror for horror's sake, although the writer of the gospel did not spare the disturbing details. Rather, this story of John's tragic fate has implications for the entirety of the gospel and for the life of faith of Jesus' disciples then and now. Keep in mind, this story comes after the sending of the twelve, perhaps as a shocking lesson of what happens to those who speak God's Word to those for whom its truth is convicting and less than lifestyle affirming. Maybe, too, this story of John's demise marks a transition in the trajectory of Jesus' story. John pointed to Jesus, prepared the way for him, and now in John's absence, Jesus' disciples must take on greater responsibilities and assume greater risk. If ever followers of Jesus thought there would be a triumphant ending to this Jesus-journey, John's fate reveals otherwise.

Certainly, this execution of John foreshadowed the crucifixion of Jesus. Even if those in power are fascinated by the word proclaimed, intrigued by the deeds of power, sympathetic to the message, and willing to note the just and holy nature of the speaker, still their loyalty to status and the need to keep the power they possess will lead to the death of

God's messenger and eventually God's son. Divine work had deadly consequences. Mark recounted the real ramifications of standing up to evil.

All this space given to tell this story demands that we sit with its ugliness and examine where we find ourselves within it.

This text calls forth a host of questions.

Who are we desperate to silence? The answer to this question may reveal the truthful Word of God we do not want to hear. If there are those we absolutely wish would keep silent, whose voices make us cringe and whose message feels like judgment, we may well want to stop and listen, despite our visceral need to shut them up.

How are we complicit in the murder of the just and holy? No one wants to answer this question. The great ones of the day, the first ones of Galilee, all they did was attend the party of Herod, and who would turn down that invitation? Even if you didn't agree with his politics or policies, he was the ruler, and what an honor to be invited, right? Who are you to speak up and say: "Hey, Herod, maybe don't do as the girl asked. Your strength could be made evident in adhering to your principles, rather than capitulating to your ego." Are those simply attending the banquet culpable for the murder of that just and holy man, John the Baptist? Surely not. They didn't have the power to intervene, and such a stand would have gotten them not only permanently blacklisted, but potentially served on a platter too.

How have we acted to save face rather than act with integrity? I'll just let you sit quietly with this one for a minute.

What actions haunt us and what do we need to do about that unease? No expansion on this needed, either.

Are we willing to point to Jesus, prepare a way for him, go to towns and villages, healing, casting out demons and proclaiming (like John) repentance? That's the marching orders the twelve got just prior to this reading for today. The cost of this mission is high: our very lives. Wouldn't we rather get a banquet invitation than sit and eat with whatever sinner offers us a seat at their paltry table?

Where do we imagine the kingdom of God is manifested — palaces, or prisons? It appeared as if Herod and Herodias were winning. They called the shots. They had the wealth. They controlled the executioner. John the Baptist's head ended up on a platter, and they lived to throw another party. Where was God's providence and power in this scenario? Mark, in devoting all this time and energy to the account of John's death, wanted to say emphatically that God's providence and power was in the prison cell, not the palace. God would work through the twelve, hardly the great ones of Galilee. God would bring the redemption of the world through the one crucified, dead, and buried. God's Word will not be silenced, despite all worldly evidence to the contrary.

It is no wonder people cannot comprehend Jesus' true identity. No wonder they can't figure out the source of Jesus' authority. No wonder they want to put this whole Jesus movement into boxes with which they are familiar. Neither they, nor we, can imagine that ultimate power could be found in prisons cells, poor people, and the condemned.

This tale of manipulation and murder foreshadowed the fate that would befall Jesus, the one neither family nor crowd could categorize. The message for the twelve, and for all disciples who came after them, is daunting: Those who wish to save their lives, will lose them. The gospel, Mark said, demands our life, our all. Speaking God's Word has real life consequences. Engaging in God's work of defeating evil doesn't gain you worldly favor. But rest assured, despite all evidence to the contrary, God's will and word will not be thwarted. If we want to be reminded of that truth, we may need to leave the palace and go instead to the prisons.

This week:

- Pray for those who are in prison. Explore the possibility of supporting a prison ministry in your area.
- When you read this story, who is culpable for John the Baptist's death? Are some more responsible than others? Why?
- Read Mark's account of Jesus before Pilate (chapter 15). Do you see connections to John's execution?

- Read Mark 13:9-13. Do we ever imagine that we will be persecuted for our faith? Do these warnings apply to us?
- This text in Mark began with John the Baptist already killed and "others" saying who they thought Jesus was. Why is this significant for the story?
- What is our relationship, as Jesus' disciples, to those with worldly power?

## Proper 11/ Ordinary Time 16

2 Samuel 7:1-14a; Ephesians 2:11-22; Mark 6:30-34, 53-56

God is on the move.

Jesus was traveling by sea and land. The Holy Spirit blew where it willed. Once you were aliens and strangers, now you are incorporated into the covenant community. The divine doesn't hunker down and doesn't allow us to remain stationary, either. Like those timers that buzz on your Fitbit, iPhone, or computer (you know, the ones that remind you to get up and move), God seems to prod us, refusing to let us get too comfortable where we are.

The king may be settled, but God told Nathan, "I have not lived in a house since the day I brought up the people of Israel from Egypt." It is almost like God got the word to King David: "Do you really think I have time to settle down and relax?! Have you looked around lately? There is work to be done! Furthermore, do you remember where you came from and where I've been with you? Why would you think I'd want to retire to temple when I relish the freedom of a tent?" David may be granted rest, but God kept moving — at least for that time.

Jesus didn't build a cedar house, either. The Son of Man had no place to lay his head. The apostles returned and told all they had done and taught — and Jesus said, "Come away to a deserted place all by yourselves and rest a while." Jesus recognized their need for rest and time apart. The needs were so great that stopping to eat wasn't an option. Clearly, an unsustainable reality, so Jesus told them to hop in the boat and get away from it all. But the crowds didn't get the memo. They went so fast on foot that they beat the apostles in the boat to the other side. They crossed over into Gennesaret and a whole host of need met them there. There were so many that the sick were brought out into the streets. Just reading about all this need makes me anxious.

God may not need a house, but I wouldn't want to live my whole life in a tent. Jesus may be able to have compassion on those who won't allow him time to eat, but I am weary of endless demands, ubiquitous suffering, and no moratorium on pain, poverty, or injustice. What is the message for me — for us — for David, the disciples, and the church in these texts? Just keep moving no matter what? Compassion fatigue is for spiritual wimps? Only the faithless need rest? I sure hope that's not the case, because if it is, I am doomed.

I have a family member who recently fell and broke her pelvis. She said in a message that she wished she could be more stoic and not scream when she moved her leg. I replied that screaming is sometimes a very appropriate response. I wanted to add, but didn't, "I scream every time I listen to the news and that feels like an appropriate response." But, really, it does. I don't think I have so much compassion fatigue as suffering overload. I care to the point I want to curl up in the corner and weep. Children are being separated from families. Refugees are denied lifesaving medical care because the border has been shut. Minors are charged as adults and held in maximum-security prisons for life. Radio shows are about the complicated drug cocktail used in executions. They are planning for how to handle the potential return of the white supremacists to my town. I have a friend in the midst of chemo. There is no justice for the people of Flint. There is another mass shooting. There is Yemen, South Sudan, and Syria.

I am not sure in this tsunami of need if I am a disciple or a member of the crowd stalking them. All I know is that I am not Jesus and I am feeling overwhelmed. Can't we just stay in the boat for a while? Hang out in a nice cedar house? Go to a deserted place? Well, yes. We can. Jesus said to the apostles who had taught and healed, traveled and shaken the dust off their feet: "Come and rest awhile. Eat. Sleep. Pray. Play. Listen to the seagulls. Rock on the waves." Jesus gave us that word, too. *Go to a deserted place by yourselves.*

As we rest, God still works. Even on the sabbath the divine order holds, the Spirit breathes, Jesus Christ prays for us, and the Triune God reigns over all the creation. Remember that truth when you want to build God a house, keep running the world's problems around your head, or you fret that sky is falling and Jesus is asleep and doesn't notice or care. The Lord of hosts is with us. The God of Jacob is our fortress. The crowds are still running before and after us. The suffering has not ceased and yet, God has not, will not abandon them or us.

Rest.

Now, get up and get moving again, because compassion won't let you wall yourself away or burn out, either. You who were once far off have been brought near through the blood of Christ, so how can you, we, not go out and bring others close, too?

The temptation (or at least my temptation) is to go off to a deserted place and stay there, wringing my hands, yes — but offering to help others with them, not so much. The verses in Mark today bracket the feeding of the 5,000. The lectionary denies us that story this week, but we know it is there. We don't get Jesus walking on water this week, either. But we know it is there. We know both that we are called to give the people something to eat and to marvel at the power of our Lord who controls even the seas and sky. That's where we rest: between human need and the promises and power of the Most High God. That's why we are able to rest. We have a purpose, a call, a role, but we are decidedly not Jesus. We not only can rest, we are commanded by our God: *You must rest.*

Rest — breathe — pray — play — look up and see the stars. Look out and see the waves. Feel the warmth of the sun. Smell the salt. Notice the beauty of the earth so that you recognize the loveliness in the faces of the needy, sometimes angry, never satisfied crowd and in yourself. Go to a deserted place. Sit down and eat so that you can get up and get moving again and feed others. The earth is the Lord's and everything in it — the ones on the mats in the marketplace, the ones running alongside the shore, the ones grabbing the hem of Jesus' garment and you, too. Rest. Rest in the promise of the covenant, rely on the strength of the community, remember that Christ is our peace and we are one body, never left solely to our own devices. We no longer have to go it alone or keep going every moment of every day. Today's worries are enough for today, so get some rest, and then get up tomorrow and know that God is already there, Jesus won't abandon you and the Holy Spirit surrounds you. I don't know about you, but that gives me hope and keeps me from screaming. At least sometimes.

This week:

- What do you do when you feel overwhelmed by the needs of the world?
- How do you find rest? What prevents you from truly resting?
- How do we want to contain God when He says, "I don't want to stay put"?
- Have you ever been in the midst of a crowd so large you couldn't move? What was that like? How do we both escape the crowd and have compassion on them?
- Where is a deserted place where you can go? Are you tempted to stay there?
- Where are other places in the gospels where Jesus is moved with pity or compassion? What moves you with compassion?

## Proper 12/Ordinary Time 17
2 Samuel 11:1-15; Ephesians 3:14-21; John 6:1-21

We do not lack for material or choices this Sunday.

The epistle this week gives us a prayer. Our Old Testament reading details King David's abhorrent behavior with Bathsheba and Uriah. The gospel lesson recounts John's version of Jesus feeding the 5,000, and then walking on water.

David's actions toward Bathsheba take on a new relevance in the era of #MeToo, and Jesus' compassion for the crowd and his subsequent instruction to the disciples to give them something to eat resonates when the headlines tell of refugees and migrants desperate for life's basic necessities. It would be easy to turn these two stories into a compare-and-contrast: Be like Jesus, don't be like David, or be more like Uriah and a lot less like David. But that reduces the Bible to a morality tale instead of the God's inspired word.

Starting with the prayer from Ephesians helps mitigate the temptation to use these stories as a warning to be good. The prayer implores that Christ dwells in our hearts by faith, that we should be rooted and grounded in love, and that we know the love of Christ moves us beyond an admonishment to behave towards the Spirit, which will shape us to be more like Christ. Remembering that sheer will alone won't help us pass the "test" of compassion and faith, knowing that Christ can do more than we hope or imagine and recalling the signs and power of Jesus puts us in our place and helps us heed the Word of the Lord, rather than work in opposition to it.

We, like David, often use our power to abuse others — perhaps not as obviously or egregiously, but nonetheless hurtful to those for whom we should have compassion. One of the challenges of both the story from 2 Samuel and the one from John is how long distance from us they may seem. We aren't as bad as David, and we can't miraculously multiply loaves and fish like Jesus. We try to treat others as we'd like to be treated and we intend to share what we have. What, therefore, do these stories of rape and murder, miracles of multiplying bread and walking on water, have to do with us?

Starting with praying the prayer of Ephesians 3:14-21, for ourselves and others points us to our need for divine intervention if we are to live in ways that reflect our knowledge of the love of Christ when we are tempted to abuse our power or when we are faced with overwhelming need. Praying this prayer moves our attention away from ourselves and toward God, opens us to following Jesus' instructions, whether we are tempted to abuse our power or feeling useless in the face of the world's needs.

May we strengthen our inner being with power through the Spirit. May Christ dwell in our hearts through faith as we are rooted and grounded in love. May we have the power to comprehend, with all the saints, what is the breadth, length, height, and depth of Christ's love and to know the love of Christ that surpasses knowledge, so that we may be filled with all the fullness of God. What if this was our daily prayer for ourselves, for our communities of faith, and for the world? Perhaps beginning with these petitions would shape how we treat Bathsheba and Uriah, the hungry crowds, the threats at sea, the use of our power, and the sharing of what we have.

An openness to the power of the Spirit and an expectation that Christ will dwell in our hearts helps us to give what we have, instead of take what is another's. Being rooted and grounded in love reveals that nothing really belongs to us anyway. An awareness of the breadth, length, height, and depth of the love of Christ inspires us to a breadth, length, height, and depth of love for others that we did not know we could extend. Being filled with the fullness of God prevents us from being too full of ourselves.

Our behavior may not be as bad as David's or as good as Jesus', but with the help of the Spirit, maybe we can be dutiful in our responsibilities like Uriah, or generous with what we have like the boy with five loaves and two fish. Through Christ dwelling within our hearts, we might be moved with compassion for the crowds rather than inclined to send them away hungry. Rooted and grounded in love, we could give what we have to God instead of grab whatever we can for ourselves. As we gain knowledge of the expansive nature of the love of God, we will no doubt experience that God can do through us more than we could ever ask or imagine, like feed 5,000 with a meager offering and even have twelve baskets left over.

When it is all too easy to get overwhelmed by the breadth of the hunger in the world, the length to which people will go to get more power, wealth and influence, the height of abuse of the vulnerable, the depth to which humanity sinks, we inevitably look at five loaves and two fish and ask with Philip, "What are they among so many people?" That's when Jesus said, "Make the people sit down." Stop and watch. Know that even when we fail the test of faith, Jesus is faithful. When we are empty, Jesus gives bread that satisfies. When we worry that there is not enough, the breadth and length and height and depth of Christ's love means that there are baskets of leftovers and nothing will be lost. And if we are struggling with imagining that such miracles are possible, we can begin with setting aside a place and time to pray.

And then, perhaps all we ask and imagine will reflect all that God asks and imagines until all are satisfied and none are lost.

This week:

- Carefully read all the accounts of the feeding of the 5,000 in the other three gospels. What differences do you notice? Are they significant?
- What is the connection between the feeding of the 5,000 and Jesus' walking on water? Why are these two stories put side by side?
- In John's gospel, the feeding of the 5,000 is one of Jesus' signs and the story points back to the wedding at Cana and forward to the resurrection appearance of Jesus eating breakfast on the beach with his disciples. Read each of these accounts. What common threads do you notice?
- Consider each person, named and unnamed, in the 2 Samuel reading and the reading from John. What can you learn from each person in each story?

- How is Jesus' test of Philip different from the Pharisees' tests of Jesus?
- When have you experienced God doing more than you could ask or imagine?

## Proper 13/Ordinary Time 18
2 Samuel 11:26-12:13a; Ephesians 4:1-16; John 6:24-35

Question-and-answer time with Jesus in John's gospel makes you want to say, "Wait, what?"

I picture a member of the crowd raising her hand, being recognized by Jesus, earnestly posing what she believed to be a straightforward question, and then scratching her head when Jesus' answer appeared unconnected to her query. Those eagerly following Jesus asked, "Rabbi, when did you come here?" Jesus, we would assume, should have answered, "Last week." Or "Last month." Or even, "I have always been here." But instead he went on a tangent about their motives for following him, saying something about them looking for bread because they were fed with the 5,000, but really they should be looking for food that endures for eternal life. *Wait, what?*

Someone else got up their courage and asked, "What must we do to perform the works of God?" Not a simple question like, "When did you come here?", but still relatively easy for this rabbi, right? Shouldn't he say, "Sell all you have and follow?" Or, "Love the Lord your God with all you heart, soul, mind, and strength and your neighbor as yourself?" Or, "Those with two coats give to those who have none?" Instead Jesus replied, "This is the work of God, that you believe in him whom he has sent." *Wait, what?*

Then the crowd got savvy. They started to regroup and revise their line of questioning, asking, "What signs are you going to give us, what work are you performing?" If we are to believe, then give us something to go on, some holy ta-da that confirms our suspicions that you are one in whom we should believe. I can't help but wonder if Jesus is the one who went, "Wait, what?" Didn't these folks just experience two loaves and five fish that turned into a feast for five thousand with baskets left over? What else did they need? But Jesus instead told them a story, one they likely knew all too well. Remember Moses? The manna and the quail in the wilderness? Yeah, that wasn't Moses' doing, that was God's.

Oh, and by the way, I am the Bread of Life, and those who believe in me will never be hungry or thirsty ever again. Any more questions?

*Wait, what?*

Q-and-A with Jesus required a lot from those posing the questions. He didn't offer easy answers even to questions that appeared to have a straightforward answer. "Rabbi, when did you come here?" Well, we know in John, in the beginning was the word. So, when did Jesus start counting? With Gabriel's announcement to Mary? With his birth? Or is it when he began his earthly ministry? Jesus instead answered the deeper questions of the crowds following him, this crowd teeming with life's most basic and most profound needs. He knew they were seeking bread, and who could blame them? Who could think of anything else when they were physically hungry, exhausted, and beaten down? Jesus knew their yearning for rest and sustenance. After all, he had compassion on them. He was not chastising them for seeking bread. He had so much more to give them than bread. This was no prosperity gospel that seduced with a message to "believe and be blessed with material things." Jesus told the crowd, hungry for food and desperate to be valued, that he offered eternal life, and in John's gospel, eternal life was abundant; it started here and now, and never ended.

Jesus didn't need them to work for that grace, he only asked them to believe. *Wait, what?* In a world then and now that is all about transactions, quid pro quo, and working the system the best you can or being crushed by it, Jesus said: "No, wait. Believe in me. You cannot earn what I offer. You can only believe and receive."

Jesus told this needy crowd for whom he had compassion: I will care for you now and forever. You are God's beloved with whom God is well pleased. God knows you need bread, but life is more than bread. Believe and receive the Bread of Life and never be hungry again.

I recently spent some time with my dad. He told me a story about my great-grandfather that I can't stop thinking about. My dad's grandfather spent much of his working life building the wooden supports for the shafts in a gold mine. He contracted a lung disease as a result. When he was too sick to work in the mines, he would take my dad and go pick blueberries to sell. My father described his grandfather with his breathing hampered, his physical strength waning, crawling on his hands and knees, picking blueberries. It helped me understand my father's relentless work ethic and inability to admit when he is tired or sick.

I imagine my great-grandfather in that crowd asking Jesus questions, one of those in need of that ordinary bread that perishes. Would Jesus fault him for following because of that hillside miracle? I don't think so. I think Jesus would have compassion for him. I think Jesus would want to offer him so much more than bread and fish. He would want to offer him an unquestionable confidence that he is not forgotten, worth more than the sum of his ability to produce, invaluable in the eyes of God. Jesus wants us to believe, so that we know God believes in our worth, beauty, and ability to contribute to the kingdom no matter our abilities, or lack thereof, in this world.

Often, we are asking Jesus questions to which he wants to answer: "Wait. You are asking the wrong questions. What I want to give you is so much more and so much better than anything you can hope, dream or imagine." We ask what works we need to do, and Jesus says it is not about works. Believe. Appreciate the signs but believe in the one who does them. Believe that God so loved the world the God sent the Son to save it, not condemn it. Believe that God calls you to be apostles, prophets, evangelists, teachers, preachers and witnesses; no matter what your job, God gives you a life-giving vocation.

We look for signs when Jesus gives us his very self. We want bread that perishes, of course, but Jesus gives his body, the Bread of Life. We want water, of course, but Jesus gives us his blood. We seek the person who satisfied our hunger, but when we believe in Jesus, the deepest longings of our hearts are sated, too.

Jesus didn't fault the crowds for looking to be fed. He had compassion on them. So much so that he didn't answer their questions. Instead he offered them life, abundant and eternal. He gave them his very self. If they could only believe it.

This week:

- What questions are you asking Jesus? How might Jesus be answering those questions with something deeper and more than you can imagine or hope?
- Do you have a difficult time accepting that works are not needed, but only belief in Jesus? Why or why not?
- What changes do you need to make to better lead a life worthy of the calling to which you have been called?
- Look up "bread" in a biblical concordance and read some of the other texts that mention bread. How do those texts color your understanding of this text from John?
- Do you think Jesus was chiding the crowd for following him because they were fed on the hillside? When do we seek Jesus out for bread that perishes?
- Take some time this week to consider when and how you came to believe in Jesus. How has your belief in Jesus changed or remained the same?

## Proper 14/Ordinary Time 19

2 Samuel 18:5-9, 15, 31-33; Ephesians 4:25-5:2; John 6:35, 41-51

Put away falsehood. Let your words give grace to those who hear. Put away bitterness and wrath, anger, slander, malice. Be kind, tenderhearted, forgiving one another as you have been forgiven. Live in love as Christ loved us.

Reading these verses from Ephesians this week elicited two reactions within me. The first and most powerful one was a deep, grief-filled longing. The second was a question: Is such a community possible? All this kindness and speech that builds up and this putting away of anger sounds too utopian to be true. I am on social media, after all. Despite my pithy plastic keychain that reads, "Never read the comments," I do, in fact, read the comments, all of them. I read Yelp reviews and watch the news, too. In these spaces, wrangling and wrath prevails.

That's why, as I read this beautiful, poetic, parenetic text from Ephesians, I was moved to tears. Be imitators of God. Yeah, right. Put away all bitterness. Sure, that'll happen. Been on Twitter lately? Let no evil talk come from you. Fat chance of that. Each admonishment seems more unrealistic, unlikely and implausible than the last. But then I read the gospel lesson appointed for this day, the one from John that continues the theme of Jesus as the Bread of Life, but this time with the skeptics and critics in the mix, the voices of those not inclined to build up others with their words or put away all wrath and bitterness. #sonofJoseph #notspecial #whodoesshethinkheis

I imagine the Twitter feed and social media accounts of those scribes and Pharisees, the ones who thought they were better than, smarter than, more than Jesus, his disciples and the crowds. I hear a familiar cynicism and self-righteousness that would fit well in our current climate, and so I lean in to hear Jesus' response to them. What did Jesus have to say to the doubters and haters?

Jesus, as was his custom, pointed to God. Always Jesus pointed to God. He reminded his hearers of their place in relation to God's power.

171

Jesus was unfazed by their complaints, aware that the gospel creates its own hearers and that God will draw to God's self those whom God calls. (Maybe eventually some of those filled with bitterness, wrath, and evil talk.) Jesus told those hell-bent on destroying, rather than building up that God's promises are not dependent upon their consent, assent or belief. Jesus' work will be done on earth as it is in heaven, with or without them. Therefore, he will continue his ministry of forgiveness, healing, salvation, and redemption, knowing that God will teach those with a teachable spirit, no matter what the haters do or say. #breadoflife #Godtaughtones #neverhunger

If that's the case, that God teaches and calls those whom God chooses, then what's the role of Christ's disciples, those of us who are preachers, teachers, followers? Be imitators of God. Be kind. Forgive as you have been forgiven. Let no evil talk come from your mouths. Start to live as if the utopian vision of Ephesians is not only possible, but promised and inevitable through the power of Christ working within us, and the Spirit blowing where it wills.

Imagine if we lived as described in Ephesians. Really, truly, daily practicing forgiveness, being kind, allowing no evil talk to come from our mouths, but only those words that build up the other, the community and the world. Would not others be drawn to us and through us, through the grace of God, to the one we follow? This vision of behavior and community in these few epistle verses this week are radically countercultural. They brought forth a longing in me that I don't think is unique to me alone. Don't we all long for such encounters and community and connection?

Those of us invested and committed to the church, the institution of the church as an expression of the Body of Christ in this world, lament readily our decline and irrelevance. We wring our hands over the loss of members and influence and, frankly, we should be concerned about such matters. That is not because we need to be large to be faithful, but because our shrinking reflects our reluctance to practice evangelism in the largest sense of that word. We have been the complainers, not the proclaimers. We have been so cynical that we've reduced Jesus to just that kid from Nazareth, rather than the Son of God who has come to save the world. Evil talk, wrangling, and wrath have spewed forth from our lips and we have failed to forgive as we have been forgiven, or love as Christ loved us.

The gospel creates its own listeners. God will draw to Jesus Christ those whom God calls. God teaches the teachable and writes God's law upon their hearts. And yet, those of us who claim to follow Jesus are called to preach and teach, too. We are called to be witnesses. We are called to go to the ends of the earth, all the world, baptizing. We are called to love God and neighbor — to tend and feed — to live a life worthy of the calling to which we have been called. We are called not just read and long for the life outlined in Ephesians, but to prayerfully, humbly, haltingly practice it every single day.

Imagine if before we fired off that comment, posted that pithy, clever post, or took out our frustration on whoever happens to be in front of us, we asked ourselves: Does this build up or does it tear down? Is this kind? Am I speaking the truth in love? How does this act or word imitate God and show the love of Christ Jesus? This is no greeting card sentiment or vapid bumper sticker or self-referential, self-help slogan. This is radical. Such practices require discipline, prayer, the ability to confess, repent, and keep trying. All these acts point away from ourselves and toward God. They demand that our focus be less inward and more outward, less skeptical and more hopeful, less fearful and more merciful, less self-righteous and more aware of our need for the grace of God, less sure of our own abilities, insight and wisdom but more open to the Spirit and God's teaching.

Imagine. No, don't imagine. Start imitating God and loving as Christ loved us, every single day. Trust that others will be drawn to us and through us, to the one we follow. No utopian vision, but the actual Body of Christ, the church.

## Lectionary Reflections

This week:

- Read through the Ephesians verses and choose one of the practices to focus on each day this week. Write down which one you intend to practice and then record your discoveries at the end of each day.
- Are you inclined to be cynical? Skeptical? Why? How do these attitudes fit or not with the message of the gospel?
- How have you been taught by God and drawn to Jesus Christ?
- John's gospel has Jesus repeating the phrase, "I am the Bread of Life." Do you think of Jesus as the Bread of Life?
- When have you been in a community that has practiced the admonitions found in this Ephesians text? When have you experienced the opposite?
- Read these other passages that talk about God teaching those whom God calls: Isaiah 54:13, Jeremiah 31:33 and 1 Thessalonians 4:9. If God is doing the teaching, what is our role?

## Proper 15/Ordinary Time 20
1 Kings 2:10-12; 3:3-14; Ephesians 5:15-20; John 6:51-58

We get more about bread this Sunday.

John, chapter 6 is long — 71 verses long. John 6 is not just long, it is dense, packed with powerhouse stories and sayings. Jesus feeds the 5,000. Jesus walks on water. Jesus says, "I am the Bread of Life" and repeatedly, "I am the bread that came down from heaven." Jesus talks of eternal life and in this Sunday's appointed verses, we are told to abide in Jesus. Next week we will finally hear from the disciples after hearing from the crowds and the Jews.

So, what's distinctive about John 6:51-58? Aren't these verses simply a reiteration of what came before? More about Jesus being the bread from heaven, the living bread, the Bread of Life, not like the manna that didn't prevent people from perishing, but something unique and available only in Jesus. More about Jews who are offended by Jesus and disputing his claims. More about Jesus' relationship to the Father. More about eternal life. What's new to say this Sunday that hasn't been said last Sunday or the one before that, or the one before that?

In some ways, nothing. These verses do repeat the themes found earlier in chapter 6. They also point further back, way further, to the exodus from Egypt and the manna in the desert as well as to Leviticus and ritual sacrifice. No doubt this bread talk is connected to the feeding of the 5,000, the five loaves, and the baskets of leftovers. They also point forward to the Last Supper, the Passover meal that remembers what God has done, and foreshadows what God is about to do through Jesus. They point forward to Jesus' death and resurrection. These few seemingly remixed verses of John point up to heaven and down to earth. There is movement here: Jesus, the bread come down from heaven. They point to Jesus, the Bread of Life who lifts up those who eat of it.

Up, down, backward, forward: these few sentences in this long chapter create a vortex of divine activity that sweep up all of creation within it, offering eternal life and an unbreakable relationship with the

Triune God. No wonder Jesus said, "Very truly, I tell you, unless you eat the flesh of the Son of Man and drink his blood, you have no life in you." Nothing short of life and death is at stake in this back-and-forth between Jesus and those who disputed his claims. Perhaps that stark truth bears proclaiming this week.

All of the bread from heaven discourse leads to this moment: Will you eat and drink and live, or not? Next week we'll find out what the disciples decide. This week, we are left to wrestle with the question for ourselves.

I imagine reading John 6:51-58 to someone who had never heard of Jesus before, and wondering what their response would be. Jesus is the bread of heaven. This bread is his flesh, his body. Eat his body, drink his blood, and you will live forever. When I think about Jesus' Words like this, I don't blame the Jews for their disputing and questioning and shock. In our context, minus our Christian tradition and experience and understanding, Jesus' claims sound like something right out of a horror movie. We need not dismiss the disgust of those Jews in John because the alternative is to clean up and sentimentalize Jesus, the bread come down from heaven, whose body and blood saves, not through a sanitized ritual but through a crucifixion.

When Jesus told his hearers to eat and drink the true food and the true drink in order to live and abide, he reminded them of the God who rescued them from slavery and invited them to follow him to the cross for the sake of the whole world. Perhaps caution about coming to this ever-expanding table is in order.

Eat, drink, live, abide, be ready to eat, drink, and abide with those you may have interacted with. Pull up a chair next to Gentiles and tax collectors, Samaritans, and all manner of sinners. Put your lips on the cup that your enemy just pressed to his mouth. Take a piece of the bread baked by the one you've feared or objectified. Jesus abides in them and we in Jesus, and all of us together with God. How unnatural this oneness of the body and blood of Jesus, this indivisible Body of Christ.

And yet, without this true food and drink, this one cup and loaf, this flesh and blood of the Son of Man, we will die. We will kill each other.

We will be left to sin and death, alienation, and separation. No wonder Jesus said, "Very truly, I tell you, unless you eat the flesh of the Son of Man and drink his blood, you have no life in you."

The manna in the desert was for God's chosen people. The bread come down from heaven was for all the nations. Eat and live forever, together, eternally, abundantly, now, and always. No more boundaries, but only one humanity. Not just the chosen are liberated and saved, but all of creation freed and redeemed. Will you eat and live? Drink and never thirst? Become a spring of living water for a parched world? Or would you rather have a walled off, private room with a reserved table and guests only on your invitation list?

Which will it be? Choose this day: life or death?

As Jesus asked his disciples in a few more verses: *Does this offend you?*

Perhaps it should. The Jews of John's gospel were right to be shocked and disgusted, dismayed and doubting, and if those emotions and thoughts don't wash over us when we read this text, then we've failed to understand what's at stake in Jesus' offering of the Bread of Life, the living bread, his flesh and blood.

The gift of Jesus, the Bread of Life, should not be received thoughtlessly nor lightly. When we eat the bread and drink from the cup we are swept into salvation history — God's past, present, and future. We make explicit the reality that our lives are not our own. We belong to God in life and in death. We abide in Jesus, who abides in God and therefore we cannot live without God nor without one another or creation. Eat, drink, and be swept up in the work of the Triune God. Eat, drink, and become a part of the one who came to serve. Eat, drink, be lifted up and poured out; be filled up and sent out. Eat and drink, pull up a seat at the table, make space for others.

Very truly, unless you eat of the flesh of the Son of Man and drink his blood, you have no life in you. So, eat your fill, drink up, and live.

## Lectionary Reflections

This week:

- Every time you encounter bread this week, consider what difference it makes that Jesus is the Bread of Life. Think about all of the scripture passages that reference bread and allow those to come to mind. How do those passages expand your understanding of Jesus as the Bread of Life?

- What does the word "abide" mean to you? How do you abide in Jesus? Read John 15:4-7 and note how it relates to these verses in chapter 6.

- Are there particularly memorable celebrations of the Lord's Supper you have experienced? What made them so?

- How would you explain the meaning of communion to someone who knew nothing about Jesus or the Bible?

- Read all of John chapter 6. How do these verses relate to the rest of the chapter?

- When you hear the expression that something was "bread from heaven," what do you think about? Does it have anything to do with Jesus as the Bread of Life?

## Proper 16/Ordinary Time 21
1 Kings 8: 22-30; Ephesians 6:10-20; John 6:56-69

Jesus asked his followers two pointed questions: Does this offend you? And: Do you also wish to go away?

He spoke plainly: I am the Bread of Life. Eat and live. I am the bread come down from heaven and this bread is my flesh. Believe, eat and receive the gift of eternal life. The Jews disputed Jesus' claim and the disciples grumbled about it.

Jesus knew their hearts and doubts and then he said it plainly: Does this offend you? Do you also wish to leave? Now is the time to turn around and head back to your former life. Many already decided that this Jesus way was not going to be their way, but what about the twelve?

I am confused about the disciples' grumbling. I do not understand, exactly, what was so difficult about this teaching. Isn't eternal life good news? Isn't bread from heaven a blessing? Isn't the promise of never hungering nor thirsting again a teaching we want to embrace?

What was so difficult and hard to accept? Was Jesus too good to be true? Was that what was difficult and nearly impossible to accept? Or did the challenge come from a place not of wonder at the gift but suspicion of the giver? Did it harken back to the beginning of John's gospel when Nathanael asked, "Can anything good come out of Nazareth?" The debate about Jesus, his identity, the source of his power and his authority remained a constant theme in John's gospel and this scene forced Jesus' followers to take a stand. Would they believe and continue to follow or were they going to turn back with so many others?

Does Jesus and his claim to be the Bread of Life come down from heaven offend you? Do you shake your head in disbelief? Are you stunned by the audacity of this carpenter from Nazareth? Is it possible for you to imagine that this poor man from an ordinary family and a backwater town could really be the one come down from heaven, sent to save the world? Don't you expect God to work through grander, more auspicious means? Feeding a bunch of needy people on a hillside is nice, but wouldn't a revolution be a more effective way of showing the world who was in charge?

That's what I want. I want Jesus to storm the palace and give those who have for too long exploited the vulnerable, lined their own pockets, and abused their positions to get what is coming to them. Instead we get bread. I don't want the distribution of life-giving bread, I want some retribution. I know I am not supposed to want that, but sometimes, I confess, I do. I may say restorative justice is the goal, forgiveness, grace and mercy, yes, of course. But when I hear of priests raping children, teenagers killed by a suicide bombers, and migrant workers rendered indentured servants, it is hard for me to accept that Jesus offers bread all around, that nothing will be left behind that can be gathered together, that Jesus has come not to condemn the world but to save it. This teaching is difficult for me. I find it hard to accept. I am offended, frankly.

There are days, far too many days, when I would rather follow a different teaching than that of Jesus Christ. I do not want to pray for my enemies. I do not want to sit at the same table with betrayers. I do not want to go to the cross. I do not want to seek reconciliation. I do not want to extend forgiveness. All of this is too difficult. Grace is offensive, but revenge far more satisfying. I want to see some people eating crow, and lots of it.

But Jesus said, *I am the Bread of Life, come down from heaven, for the sake of the world.* Not everyone will believe, many will be offended, but for those who eat and drink, they will live, differently, fully, abundantly and for the sake of the world, too.

Do you also wish to turn away?

Sometimes I do, because grace is hard to stomach when it is extended to those I want to get what I think is coming to them. Not only that, but eating this bread from heaven requires that I am what I eat, that I abide in Jesus, that I put on the whole armor of God and take on the cosmic powers of this present darkness, that I offer heavenly bread indiscriminately and eat with anyone and everyone.

Recently, in the free paper that lists upcoming events and features articles on local happenings in my city, the question posed on the next to last page was this: "How does your faith get you through difficult times?" The answers ranged from "I have no religious faith whatsoever, and never have. This helps me get through difficult times because I don't expect the celestial cavalry to suddenly come and rescue me. Instead, I depend on my own wits and experience," to "Whenever I need to find a being greater than myself, more valuable to the world than myself, all I need so is look to the trees." And then this: "Christ Jesus has been the great answer to everything in my life in the last thirty years. He is totally real, and he's 100% love. It's easy — just invite him in. No risk and no downside, I promise!"

While I do not agree with the first two responses, it is the third, the one about Jesus, that troubles me the most. "It's easy." And, "No risk and no downside." Really? Somehow this follower missed the offensive, scandalous, take-up-your-cross, lose-your-life part of following Christ Jesus. Jesus sounds like the latest gadget being proffered on late night television infomercials, not the Messiah who came to serve and pour himself out to the point of death on a cross. One might as well look to the trees or rely on one's wits if the One we follow requires nothing of us but our invitation. So much for God doing the calling, teaching, and choosing.

When we forget the offense and difficulty of Jesus' teachings, we fail to recognize that there is nowhere else to go for eternal life. We reduce the bread from heaven to some sort of magic beans that grant our wishes. We turn the Bread of Life into comfort food that confirms the status quo, and Jesus gives his body that we might be salt and light and leaven in the world.

Abiding with the One who came from Nazareth inevitably puts us in the company of those we do not choose. Eating the Bread of Life incorporates us into the Body of Christ and calls us to be dependent upon and concerned for every member of it. Hearing the word of the Spirit means going where it wills. Believing that Jesus is the Messiah requires that we follow his teachings, difficult and offensive as they are. Does this offend you? Perhaps it should.

This week:

- Do you find Jesus' teachings difficult? Are you ever offended by Jesus?

- Have you ever turned away from Jesus or been tempted to do so? To whom did you go? What caused you to turn back?

- The letter to the Ephesians says that we are up against the "cosmic forces of this present darkness" and "the spiritual forces of evil." Do you ever think about a life of faith in this way?

- Read the verses from Ephesians and make a list of what the "whole armor of God" entails. Can you think about being equipped with these things throughout your daily living? What difference does it make to be aware of wearing the "whole armor of God?"

- Jesus knows his disciples are complaining about his teachings. What are we complaining about in the church? In our lives? How might Jesus respond to our grumbling?

- How would you answer this question: How does faith get you through difficult times?

## Proper 17/Ordinary Time 22
James 1:17-27; Mark 7:1-8, 14-15, 21-23

What matters in a life of faith? Which is more important: following prescribed rituals or practicing right conduct? What parts of our daily living set us apart and reveal our loyalties?

These questions come up again and again in scripture. Jesus said that not everyone who says "Lord, Lord" will enter the kingdom. What counts, Jesus said, is doing the will of God. The prophets are not silent on these matters, either. The prophets told their hearers that God proclaimed, "I hate and despise your feasts." The people's worship did not bring God joy because the very ones praising God were exploiting the widows and orphans. Jesus ended the debate about what was lawful on the sabbath with the proclamation that the sabbath was made for humanity, not the other way around. Oh, and by the way, he said, "I desire mercy and not sacrifice."

What is critical to God if we are to be faithful disciples of Jesus Christ? If our diet does not mark us strange and our dress is indistinguishable from others, what reveals our allegiance to Jesus? What is distinctive about us?

James, that book of the Bible not beloved by the reformers, says that we must be doers of the word, not merely passive hearers. James, too closely associated with works righteousness for some, says that undefiled religion is caring for widows and orphans in distress. For James, this is the non-negotiable of faith.

That passage so often read at weddings (no, not Song of Solomon), 1 Corinthians 13, states that speaking in tongues, prophetic powers, understanding, and knowledge are nothing — they render us nothing — without love, patience, kindness, and endurance.

In other words, clean hands are nothing without a pure heart and the actions that spring forth from it.

It would be easy to take these texts from James and Mark this week and conclude that nothing other than our actions matter, that worship is optional, ritual overrated, tradition meaningless, belief less important than works. It is tempting to use this week's readings as a means of jettisoning anything about our congregations or current practices that we do not like or just long to change. Mid-week Bible study? We should be out feeding the hungry instead. Worship? Let's spend that time in mission. In the words of Isaiah quoted by Jesus, we need to make sure we aren't honoring God with our lips but keeping our lives and hearts off limits.

The last thing we want to be is a white-washed-tomb Pharisee, so let's ditch tradition and get to work, pronto.

Creating that kind of dichotomy is simple. A life of faith, however, is complicated. Living with integrity, having the words of our lips match the actions of our hands, our professed beliefs align with our day to day decisions — that's hard. Hence, we need tradition, ritual, worship, and prayer — all the things that can become empty, meaningless, rote, or hypocritical if they don't shape our character and become evident in our choices.

Keep in mind that this story comes in Mark just after Jesus had been lauded in a Jewish part of the world, and was about to embark on a major mission to the Gentiles. This hand-washing question is not theoretical to those who are asking it and Jesus' answer has consequences for his ministry and that of his disciples. This question about tradition is bigger than righteous rule-following; this is about expanding membership in the family of God. This isn't really about whose hands are dirty, it is about which people we name as unclean. Jesus was not saying to jettison all the law, he said he had come to fulfill it after all. He was giving notice to the Pharisees and any others who wanted to limit God's grace, concern, and community, that no ritual, tradition, or religious practice should be used to constrain the will and work of the Most High.

And yet, Jesus went to the synagogue regularly, as was his custom. He quoted scripture. He prayed. He went to Jerusalem for Passover. It seems the tradition of the elders was of critical importance to Jesus, so much so that even the Son of Man practiced those traditions. The question these readings beg is not: Do religious rituals matter? The question is: What is the point of doing these religious rituals?

First and foremost, they put us in our place. They enact the truth that we have no other gods before our God. They mark and make us different. We head to worship on Sunday morning, driving past packed coffee houses, busy parks, and booming strip malls. Our worship bears witness to the world that there is another rhythm and rule than consumerism. Our liturgy tells an alternative story about where people's worth is to be found and why each person matters. Our scripture reveals a plot, counter to the one of death and destruction constantly being broadcast everywhere else. These traditions, through the power of the Spirit and the grace of God, shape us into those worthy of the calling to which we have been called, and when they don't, they offer a means to confess, repent, and try again.

Jesus did not tell the crowds that rituals did not matter, that the tradition of the elders was insignificant or wrong-headed; he told the Pharisees and the crowd that those practices were not ultimate. God alone was ultimate. Jesus said that those God-given means of grace mock God when those who practice them do not enact them in their daily living. Jesus said that when those traditions are used as an excuse to exclude or abuse, marginalize or ridicule, they enrage the God they are designed to glorify.

As Jesus prepared to go to the Gentiles, he made it unequivocally clear to the Pharisees, the crowds, and his disciples: Nothing God ordained will prevent them from sitting at table together. Those who were once far away will be brought close — not because Jesus came to abolish the law, but because he came to fulfill it.

Clean hands mean nothing if the one who has washed doesn't also have a cleansed heart and a right spirit within them. Through the grace of God, may we be those whose lips and words, hearts and hands, match our actions.

This week:

- How do you understand the role of tradition, ritual, and religious practices?

- The earliest Christians had to wrestle with real questions about which religious practices were essential and which could be changed or ignored so that the community could be one. How is this still true?

- How has Christianity evolved in your lifetime? What has changed? What has remained unchanged? How did those changes come about?

- Aren't we all hypocrites? Given that all sin and fall short of the glory of God, how do we live with integrity despite our inevitable mistakes and shortcomings?

- These verses from James instruct us to be quick to listen, slow to speak and slow to anger. Does this describe you? How can you practice James' instructions?

- How are you and your faith community practicing "undefiled religion" by caring for "orphans and widows in distress?"

**Proper 18/Ordinary Time 23**

Proverbs 22:1-2, 8-9, 22-23; James 2:1-17; Mark 7:24-37

The texts for this Sunday are Christianity 101, perhaps better known as basic instructions for being a decent human being.

Don't exploit the poor and vulnerable. Don't treat people differently based on wealth, status, power or influence they may have. If someone is hungry, feed them. Don't call a person who is desperate for help for her child a dog (yes, that's a good piece of advice on the decency for dummies list).

And yet, looking around our world and no less into our own hearts, we know that just because something is basic it doesn't mean it is easy. Christianity 101, Human Decency 1.0, requires lifelong learning that includes apprenticeships, communal accountability, practice, repentance and lots of trial and error.

Given that reality, let's go over some basics based on this Sunday's readings:

1. God created everyone — every single person. We have that in common no matter our other myriad of differences.

2. Integrity is more valuable than material wealth in the eyes of God. Therefore, always choose a good name over great riches. (Um, that might be a timely word, friends.)

3. The Lord pleads the case of the poor. Ergo, so should we.

4. Generosity is a blessing all around, for the giver and the receiver.

5. Don't exploit the poor. (There are many examples to list how the poor are exploited: title loans, cash bail, prison labor, subprime loans, higher prices on groceries in food deserts. The list is very, very long. Do a little digging into the policies and systems in your community, pick a few and hold them up in contrast to Christianity 101 this week.)

6. A person's value does not equate to their monetary net worth. A person is valuable because, well, see number one on this list. God does not care how much or how little is in your bank account. See number two on this list.

7. Love your neighbor as yourself — really. Not in theory, but in daily, tangible practice. See number five for more information.

8. Faith is visible to all. How we live reflects our deepest beliefs, revealing what and who we truly value. (Please don't go to lunch after worship, clearly having been to church, and treat the server badly or leave a meagerly tip. Please, just don't.)

9. When someone comes to you in pain and suffering, at the very least treat them with dignity, respect and kindness, even if you cannot do for him what he hopes you can do.

10. When someone comes to you in pain and suffering, do what you can do to alleviate their pain and suffering, no matter who they are, where they comes from or how that pain and suffering came to be.

A top-ten list feels like a good place to start. Let's call this "Discipleship for Dummies: A Top-Ten List of Basic Instructions." Okay, this title violates the "don't-call-people-names" rule. Let's try again: "Christianity 101: A 10-point Catechism." Or how about a more academic spin: "Practicing Parenesis in a Post-Christian Context." (Oh, I like that one!)

This gospel reading always makes me uneasy because Jesus came across as dismissive and mean-spirited. I don't like to think of Jesus this way. There is enough dismissive and mean-spiritedness around. I need Jesus to be anything but dismissive and mean-spirited. And yet, I can't just give my Lord a pass on this troubling exchange, and I refuse to believe he was just providing some sort of role-play lesson to his disciples at the expense of this woman. The fact is, it is more helpful to me to read this passage, and the healing right after it, as demonstrating Jesus' growth in compassion. I want Jesus to be changed because of his encounter with the person heretofore he did not think he had any obligation to care about, tend to or help. I find hope in seeing transformation on the part of the One who came to save the world. Even Jesus had to learn to live into the expansive, boundary-busting, salvific work of God. And if Jesus expanded his heart and subsequent actions, and God is always doing a new thing, and the Spirit blows where it wills, then I can better believe that dismissiveness, mean-spirited, exploitive, cruel, or dehumanizing acts are not inevitable, eternal, irreversible, pervasive, or relentless as they are.

I am reading *The Color of Law* by Richard Rothstein. Rothstein recounts instance after painful instance of systematic, intentional, evil housing discrimination against African Americans. Reading this book helped me understand Katie Cannon's statement, quoting her grandmother, at a lecture at Princeton in 2017, "Even when they lie, they lie." The layers and insidiousness of exploitation and abuse boggle my mind. (I know they don't surprise my friends and neighbors who have experienced this over and over again; My white privilege is showing.) Government on all levels, neighborhood associations, builders, insurance companies and, yes, churches actively participated in making sure African Americans did not have access to housing and that segregation persisted long after courts ruled it illegal.

Rothstein, writing about restrictive covenants crafted to keep African Americans out of white neighborhoods, said, "Churches, synagogues, and the clergy frequently led such efforts." One white owners' group in St. Louis was sponsored by a Presbyterian Church. "Trustees of the church provided funds from the church treasury to finance the … lawsuit to have the African American family evicted…. Such church involvement and leadership were commonplace to property owners' associations that were organized to maintain neighborhood segregation."

Basic Christianity, basic human decency, is not so basic — not when Proverbs, James, or Mark was written, not now, or ever. Christianity 101 requires intentional lifelong learning and the willingness to be held accountable by one another, yes, and surely by God. Even Jesus needed a refresher course, taught by a Syrophoenician woman. I wonder who is trying to school us right now. Are we willing to learn? Are we willing to expand our compassion and change our actions?

This week:

- Where do you see people being treated differently based on their perceived wealth, status, or power? Do you see this in the church? When have you shown partiality?
- James asked: Can faith save us? Don't reformed Christians answer "yes" to this question? What do we do with James' claim that faith without works is dead?
- What is the relationship between the two healings in the reading from Mark? What is the point of the secrecy in Jesus' healing of the deaf man?
- What about the Syrophoenician woman's response prompted Jesus to heal her daughter? In the Matthew version of this story, Jesus said the woman's faith had made her well. What is the significance of that being omitted in Mark's version? Read Matthew 15:21-28 and note the differences between the two accounts.
- How are the poor exploited in your community? How is your congregation called to respond?
- If you had to create a "top-ten" list of marks of a Christian, what would that list include?

Proper 19/Ordinary Time 24
Proverbs 1:20-33; James 3:1-12; Mark 8:27-38


Wisdom cries out in the street, mostly unheard as those within earshot hate knowledge and neglect the fear of the Lord.

James admonished us to control our tongues, asked how it is that we Christians could bless the Lord and then curse those made in the likeness of God. Jesus wanted to know what people were saying about him and, more to the point, who his followers thought he was. This Sunday requires some boldness on the part of preachers and teachers, because the biblical texts for the week won't let any of us off the hook. Scripture is calling us out for failing to have ears that hear the Word of the Lord. It is admonishing us for speaking in ways that don't reflect the character or will of our God. It is rebuking us for attempting to prevent the Messiah from fulfilling his mission. Whatever happened to *Jesus loves me, this I know*?

Jesus does, in fact, love us, but that doesn't mean Jesus commends our every thought, word, or deed. Jesus loves us enough to call us out. Jesus loves us enough to call us beyond ourselves. Jesus loves us enough to give all of himself for our sake and invite us to give all of ourselves for his sake and for the sake of the gospel. How about instead we just sing a few nice hymns, put a couple of dollars in the plate, and head out for a leisurely lunch and a lazy Sunday afternoon?

Who signs up to hear the news that we no longer live to ourselves, that even before a word is on our lips God knows it and expects it to reflect our love and loyalty to the Lord? Who wants to hear that our ways are not those of God and therefore we need to check our instincts and see if they square with wisdom's call? All of this sounds as if we are called to deny ourselves. Really — deny ourselves. Put the brakes on our tongues and thumbs, our speech and tweets. Question our justifications about our status, wealth, and power. Consider who we say that Jesus is and start examining if our lives reflect that confession of faith. Take up our cross and follow — seriously.

No wonder Peter balked right after he blurted out the truth of Jesus' identity. "You are the Messiah," Peter said. And Jesus began to teach them what that would entail in the coming days: suffering, rejection, death, resurrection. He said this "quite openly." That's when Peter said, "No way, Jesus. Not happening. Not you. Not this. Not if I have anything to do with it." Peter, like us, didn't want this kind of Messiah. Peter didn't want his friend to suffer and die. If this is what it meant to be the Messiah, forget it. Isn't it enough that John the Baptist was beheaded? Elijah fares okay, but most of the prophets didn't exactly get a fairy-tale ending. Surely the Messiah didn't have to experience such an ignominious fate as rejection and death? Certainly the Messiah got to skip over the suffering and go directly to glory, right?

Peter wanted better for Jesus and like us, wanted better for himself too. We want Jesus to be anything other than the servant Lord and the crucified Savior. We want him to be the wish-granting hero of the prosperity gospel. We want him to be the confidant cozied up to those in power. We want him to be a good example to emulate and evoke at our convenience, or maybe the nice, gentle shepherd who loves us just the way we are, no matter how we are or what we do. We don't want a mocked, rejected, suffering Messiah who tells us to take up our cross and follow, but Jesus tells us quite openly: "Those who want to save their life will lose it, and those who lose their life for my sake, and for the sake of the gospel, will save it."

But what does that mean? Even if we want to deny ourselves, and take up our crosses and follow, what does that look like? If we say Jesus is the Messiah, more than a prophet like John the Baptist, who was a moral teacher, a nice person, or a granter of our greatest desires, but rather see him as the one who was rejected, suffered, died, and was raised on the third day, what does that matter for our daily living? For our church? For our world?

At base, our confession of faith and our desire to live a life reflective of the One we say we follow means that our lives are not our own. In life and in death, we belong to God. We are not the masters of our own fate or makers of our own stories, as appealing as our culture tries to make that narrative sound. Nor are we pawns in some cosmic chess game. We are children of God, disciples of Jesus, members of the Body of Christ. A royal priesthood consists of salt, light, sheep, and witnesses. We are stewards of the mystery of God and scribes of the kingdom. We are adopted, engrafted members of the holy household. That's who we are. That's who we are because Jesus is the Messiah. Nothing can separate us from the love of God anymore. Once we've been found, what do we possibly have to lose except our lives, for the sake of our Savior and the Gospel?

If we acted with just a fraction of that abandon and confidence, our lives and the world would be radically different. People would be more important than property values. Love would triumph over fear. Mercy, not retribution, would be our default mode. Humility would replace hubris. Generosity would smother greed with its goodness. Wisdom's cries would be accompanied by choruses of praise. Even the rocks would shout out in joy. Demoniacs would no longer be relegated to graveyards. Prodigal parties would rage on every single night, and no one would be left injured by the side of the road.

If followers of Christ embraced the truth that once you've been found, you have nothing to lose, we could really live it up together.

This week:

- How do you describe what it means to deny yourself, take up your cross and follow?
- James gives a lot of power to speech and words. Is that an accurate attribution of power? How much do our words, written and spoken, matter? What impact do they have?
- Who do we, as a culture, say that Jesus is? Who do you, through your actions and choices, say that Jesus is?
- Why did Jesus equate Peter with Satan? Where else in scripture did Jesus tell Satan to go packing?
- Proverbs said the people did not "choose fear of the Lord." What does it mean to fear the Lord? How do we choose "fear of the Lord" or not?
- What is wisdom crying out in our streets? Are we listening?

## Proper 20/Ordinary Time 25
James 3:13-4:3, 7-8a; Mark 9:30-37

They didn't know what Jesus was saying, but they were afraid to ask him what he meant.

How many times have we been afraid to ask — even when we knew we didn't understand? How often has our fear of revealing our ignorance prevented us from a revelation, from a new way of seeing, from a deepened relationship? We know the saying "There are no stupid questions," and yet we do not ever want to *appear* stupid. It takes courage to raise our hand, stop the lecture, risk the annoyance of the teacher, face the eye rolls of our fellow students and say: "I have no idea what you are talking about."

Most of us can recall being shamed for a lack of understanding or knowledge and that feeling is never far from the surface of our consciousness. Hence, we are afraid to ask. Subsequently, we act out of our unknowing and only deepen misunderstanding and mistakes. We coast and bluff through algebra only to be totally overwhelmed in calculus. (Or was that just me?) We fake it until we can no longer make it. All because we are afraid to ask — even to ask Jesus.

Does it surprise you that the disciples, at this point in the story, were afraid to ask Jesus what he meant? At this point in story, they had heard Jesus preach, seen Jesus heal, been exposed to parables, and even experienced Jesus still the storm — and yet, they were still afraid. Why were they fearful and of what were they afraid? What would have been the harm in saying: "Jesus, we don't understand what you are talking about? Why all this gloom and doom? How is it that you can be killed and then rise again?" These were legitimate questions. Would Jesus really fault them for not understanding?

But none among them voiced the questions all of them had. Not even Peter blurted out his confusion. Instead they bickered about who was the greatest. Obviously, they didn't understand what Jesus was saying. He was talking about suffering and death. They were debating glory, power, and status. They needed clarification, correction, and further instruction. And so do we.

We get this Jesus-following all wrong, too. We see our relationship with Jesus as instrumental, a means to a glorious end. We want a ticket to legitimacy, deference, or moral superiority. Even in our post-modern, post-Christian culture, we imagine that claiming closeness to Jesus offers an avenue to greatness, even if only in our own estimation. I cannot help but think of ministers who abuse children, pastors who relish closeness to secular powers, church leaders who make statements divorcing social justice from the gospel, Christians who condemn people of other faiths, and disciples who tout saving souls even while subjugating others. We have no idea what Jesus was saying, and we are afraid to ask because asking requires hearing and heeding Jesus' answers.

Jesus knew, even before asking, what his disciples were arguing about then and now. He knows we are vying for greatness. We like being great. We want to be great again and always, no matter who pays the price for our greatness measured in how much power and money we amass. James reminds us that wisdom and understanding are marked by gentleness, peace, mercy, a willingness to yield, no partiality or hypocrisy. It looks like a child: welcomed, loved, cared for, and protected. Understanding Jesus — what he says, who he is — is evident in how we treat the least, not in being great. Any questions?

As I drive to my office I often pass numerous people standing on street corners holding up cardboard signs that read: "Anything helps" and "Willing to work" or "Please help." One gentleman waved at passing cars while holding up a poster board that said, "Smile, it's not that bad." One person I pass with regularity is elderly and slight; he looks defeated. When I see him, I think about the fact that he was once someone's baby, utterly vulnerable, and I so hope, totally beloved. Now he appears utterly vulnerable and certainly totally beloved by God. But here he stands or sits on a blue plastic milk crate, pleading for help. I don't understand why, but I do not ask questions that might require something of me.

There is a younger man whose corner is near a major university. He has no legs. He sits on the ground, his wheelchair behind him, his sign propped in his lap. School is back in session, the sidewalks teeming with twenty-somethings. As I sit at the light waiting for it turn green, I see most students walking briskly around him. But then I notice a young man stop. The two are talking. Then the student moves behind the wheelchair, putting his hands on the handles. He stands patiently, bracing the wheelchair, as the man with no legs heaves himself into the chair and tucks his sign behind his back. The two of them head down the sidewalk, still talking. It seems to be a work done with gentleness, a simple act of mercy that revealed an understanding of the kind of greatness Jesus taught. It struck me due to its rarity.

Sometimes I don't ask questions — not because of what I don't know, but because of what I do know, but want to pretend I don't. I understand all too well Jesus' teaching that his followers are called to be servants. I understand all too well that disciples of Jesus Christ are to welcome children, care for the least, seek out the lost and cast their lot with the suffering. Too often, though, I drive by, doors locked, radio on, unwilling to stop and ask questions because the answers will require something of me, something counter to the worldly greatness I seek. I say I don't know what to do when, really, I know I am to do something. Something gentle, merciful, peaceable. I understand what it means to welcome children. Unlike the twelve, I know what Jesus meant when he said in three days he would rise again. But instead of asking pointed questions and demanding answers, I keep quiet, fain ignorance, and strive to be great, lost in selfish ambition, allowing disorder and wickedness to run wild.

The light turns green at the top of the hour, the news comes on the radio, the reporter tells of record numbers of migrant children being kept in detention and "overwhelming the system." Maybe I should speak up, ask questions, demand answers, do something born of gentleness and mercy until wisdom, understanding and welcome win. Wouldn't that be great?

This week:

- Why were the disciples afraid to ask Jesus what he meant? Are there questions we really don't want the answers to?

- James asked: Who is wise and understanding among you? Are there people you think are wise and understanding? What makes them so?

- How do we welcome children in Jesus' name? In church? In our communities? In the world?

- Does Jesus really want us to be a "servant of all"? What does that look like?

- When has your fear of asking a question led to greater ignorance, mistakes, or problems? When have you risked asking a question even when you were reluctant to do so? What happened?

- Why do we want to be the greatest? What does it mean to you to be the greatest?

## Proper 21/Ordinary Time 26
Esther 7:1-6, 9-10; 9:20-22; James 5:13-20; Mark 9:38-50

Esther, elders, unknown exorcists: Who has the authority to speak on behalf of God for the sake of God's people?

All three texts this week revolve around the role of human beings in advocating, angling, and agitating for God's will to be done. Esther petitioned the king to spare her people. James admonished faith leaders to pray for the sick and suffering among them. Jesus told the antsy disciples to let those outside the inner circle cast out demons in his name. The boundaries on who is commissioned for divine duty are porous, expansive, and unexpected.

Everyone — those living in the palace, those gathering in humble house churches, and strangers we encounter praying and prophesying on the street — will be enlisted into the service of the Lord. Those of us close to Jesus must not attempt to contain the Spirit. Disciples of Jesus Christ should, at the very least, stay out of the way and, at our very best, make straight a path in the wilderness for the coming of our God.

Jesus said, "Whoever is not against us if for us." In a climate in which we are constantly evaluating who agrees with us, who aligns with our thinking, who checks off all the boxes of righteousness, and rightness, these Words of Jesus are no less radical that when he calls us to love our enemies and pray for those who persecute us or to sell all we have and lose our lives. Those who are not against us are for us. No one who does a deed of power in Jesus' name will be able to speak evil of him. If someone even gives you a cup of water as you go about the work of the Lord, they will not lose their reward.

Jesus' reward and regard come to those not necessarily in our pews or on our side; they come to those standing up to evil, providing for people's basic needs and making a way for the wholeness God desires for all of creation. In other words: those on Jesus' side. The Esthers who use their positions and privilege on behalf of the vulnerable and persecuted. They are the faith leaders who confess their own sin, forgive others, and pray for the suffering. They are the outsiders who call on the name of Jesus to fell the demonic and hand out cups of water to the thirsty. Shouldn't we rejoice in this truth? Why do we resist God's choice, ability, and will to work through whomever God chooses? Why do we put up barriers to keep others from God when God in Christ came to obliterate these very divisions? Why do we choose stumbling blocks over saltiness?

I confess that I have been like Jesus' disciples: anxious that orthodoxy was being breached, process circumvented, decency and order neglected. If there are not rules and requirements in this life of faith, how can a life of faith be meaningful, substantive, or followed? There should be baptism before you get a seat at the Lord's table, and membership if you want to be married in the church. What about secular music, movie clips, and Ted Talks? Not in Sunday morning worship, thank you very much. Jesus, someone is casting out demons in your name, but he doesn't follow us (or our norms, expectations, timing, dress code, methods)! But rest assured, we did our best to put a stop to it!

We expect Jesus to give us a pat on the back for keeping everything between the lines we paint, but Jesus said: "Wait a minute. Whoever is not against us is for us. You don't get to choose who does my will. That's God's call. Stop putting stumbling blocks in the very places the Spirit is blazing the way."

Jesus was serious about this admonition. Cut off your hand or foot. Put out your eye. Do whatever it takes to keep yourself from being a scandalous hindrance to the work of the Lord. Better to be maimed than thrown into the unquenchable fires of hell. Don't lose your saltiness for the sake of the status quo. If you have access to the king, speak up for those being crushed by the empire. If you have been set apart to lead, be the first to confess your failings and forgive those of others. If you witness demons being felled, join the ones doing the slaying. If you see someone who is parched, withering or dying for relief, give them water to drink and offer the water of life that overflows. Rejoice when you are given a cup to slake your thirst. Make sure the rules are road signs that point the way, not barricades that trip you up and cause everyone else around you to fall.

I attended a panel discussion with three Christian authors and after their presentation, I asked: How do we welcome those not inside our churches (the number of whom is growing rapidly), while maintaining the structure, theology, and doctrine that makes us distinct? One of the scholars, a historian, said, "We've had 2,000 years of orthodoxy in one form or another, so I'm not too worried about its sticking power. I'm more concerned with being flexible enough to reach those on the margins." She put me in my place and I was grateful she did.

While I do believe tradition, doctrine — and, yes, orthodoxy — are important and we disciples should know our theology and be able to articulate it, I have come to believe that caring for little ones is more important. Our challenge is to choose saltiness over stumbling blocks, prayer over pontificating, speaking up over personal safety, standing up to evil over circling the wagons and living water instead of dusty, well-trodden paths. Better to get rid of my own hand, foot or eye than put up barriers that prevent another from knowing the love, justice, grace, mercy and peace of Jesus Christ.

In his book "Incarnational Ministry: Being with the Church," Samuels Wells wrote, *God is bigger than you think, and you are a bigger part of what God has in mind than you currently imagine.* Just look at Esther and the elders and all of those combatting evil, casting out demons, passing out cups of water, and shaking salt all over the earth.

This week:

- What 'causes you to stumble'? What does it mean to stumble in this passage from Mark?
- When have you struggled with following policy, rules or tradition versus being open to a "stranger" casting out demons?
- How do we discern between the new thing God is doing and maintaining religious practices? How does scripture help us with this discernment?

- Where do you have power and influence? How are you called to use your power and influence on behalf of those without such privilege?
- Does your church practice what James instructs in chapter 5:13-20? When have you gathered to pray on behalf of a sick or suffering member?
- Do you believe that whoever is not against us is for us? What does that look like in our daily lives?

## Proper 22/Ordinary Time 27
Job 1:1, 2:1-10; Hebrews 1:1-4, 2:5-12; Mark 10:2-16

"There once was a man…"

Job began like a fable or fairytale: Once upon a time, in a land far, far away, there was a blameless man who feared God. We know this set-up, something out of the ordinary is about to happen to this man, a journey, a test, an unexpected encounter. Nothing will be the same for this blameless and upright man, so we lean in and anticipate the roller coaster ride of the story.

The same is true for the Hebrews text: "Long ago, God spoke to our ancestors…" Gather around everyone, and hear the story you know so well, told again so that none of us forget. Hear it again so that the moral, instruction, encouragement, or promise becomes your own and that of the next generation and the next and the next. Once upon a time, the prophets spoke and in these days — these last days — God has spoken through the Son, so lean in and listen for the timeless wisdom and will of our Lord.

Then Mark gave us the classic set-up for a showdown between Jesus and those who oppose him: "Some Pharisees came to test him…" And we know what's coming. We know it will be a back-and-forth between the reign of God and the rules and ruler of this world. We know, ultimately, that God's kingdom will come, on earth as it is in heaven. But right now, in these days, we lean in and listen for the Word of the Lord for us, right now, in tumultuous and challenging times.

All three of these appointed texts call us to attention with the familiarity of favorite childhood stories and the drama of good versus evil, and the anxious hope of knowing the ending while simultaneously living our own unique journey to get there.

So, lean in and listen, for the Word of the Lord, about a man named Job, about the proclamation of the prophets about Word incarnate in the Son and resisted throughout the ages.

Lean in and listen about integrity, that elusive trait, priceless and yet all too easily and cheaply sold for a little more money or a little more power or status or adulation or self-protection. Hear the Word of the Lord that bellows through all creation: persist in your integrity. As the introduction to the Declaration of Barmen reminds believers, test everything against scripture. If what we claim is contrary to the Word of Lord, they wrote, discard it. If, however, our story matches God's, then stop at nothing and pay whatever price is required to follow this narrative. Persist in your integrity: the integrity of discipleship. Love the Lord with all your heart, soul, mind and strength and your neighbor as yourself. Worship the Lord your God, no matter your circumstances. There once was a man, believers, who persisted in his integrity, on one day and every day. Will you?

Lean in and listen in these days about the last days and the first days, about the in-the-beginning days and the there-will-come-a-day, about Jesus Christ. Remember the stories that tell of the One who sustains all things through his powerful word, no matter the rhetoric you are hearing. Don't forget that this Son, this One, made purification for our sins, once and for always, no matter what happens on any given day. Jesus is with us, in our suffering, in the chaos of sickness and the relentless, systematic march of oppression. Look for Jesus and keep in mind that God is mindful of human beings, bringing everything to glory. Can you see it?

Lean in and listen, gather around close, and hear again about Pharisees testing the Son of God, the One sent to save. Take a seat and witness the Word made flesh fulfill the law and make all things new, too. Learn what the Lord requires of us in our household and in the cosmos. Picture those who've come to test the Lord of all. They came with an agenda and a plan, a trick question, a test that they knew Jesus can only fail: "Is it lawful for a man to divorce his wife?" Jesus answers with his own question: "What did Moses command you?" And these Pharisees know better than anyone what Moses said. Moses allowed it if a wife displeased a husband, she could be dismissed. Jesus nodded and added, "Yes, because of your hardness of hearts, but I say to you, those God has joined together let no one separate." Jesus took the religious righteous back to the in the beginning intentions of a good and gracious God.

The will of God who created and called us good is union not schism, community not estrangement, compassion not heartlessness. Women, Jesus said, are not to be discarded, discounted, demeaned, or dismissed. Children too, are precious to the Most High God. Jesus got indignant, furious, at his twelve disciples who prevented the children's blessings. The kingdom of God belongs to these very little ones they were dismissing, discarding, discounting, and demeaning. Those whom God has created, called good, loved enough to send God's Son to save, do not ever, ever, shun and shame, ignore or abuse. The kingdom of God is theirs.

Once upon a time there was a God, who sent the Son to save the world. God so loved the world, in fact, that Jesus Christ came to serve, poured himself out, and died a painful and humiliating death to defeat sin, death, and evil. In those days, Jesus stood up to every test and fulfilled every letter of the law showing those who believed and those who refused to hear that God desires mercy, not sacrifice. In these days, the Word still speaks, sustaining us with its power, infused with the Spirit.

Lean in and listen, for once upon a time is this time, our time, all time — and God refuses to remain silent and commands us to speak up, too. Hear and proclaim the Word and will of God: Persist in your integrity, love God with all you've got, and love your neighbor as well. Put no other gods before your God, no matter the cost. Never forget that God is mindful of humanity, with us in our suffering, ever combatting evil and bringing about justice. Get yourself back up and gird your loins whenever the vulnerable are sold for a piece of silver, trampled on by the powerful, categorically dismissed, discarded, discounted, or demeaned. Women matter and deserve to be heard and believed. The kingdom of God belongs to children.

Do our words reflect the Word? Do our actions heed the Spirit? Do our communities shine the light of Christ? In these days and in future ones, what will come after 'There once was a church...'?

This week:

- When has it been challenging to persist in your integrity? What does it mean to have integrity as a disciple of Jesus Christ?
- Was Job's wife justified in calling on Job to "curse God and die"? Was this an act of faith or faithlessness?
- Read Psalm 8, quoted in the Hebrews text, and consider what it means that God is mindful of human beings. What does it mean that God has crowned us with glory and subjected things under our feet?
- What do you see as the relationship between the discussion of divorce and the encounter with little children? Why does the writer of Mark's gospel put these stories side by side?
- Notice in verse ten of the Mark text that once the disciples and Jesus are "in the house," the disciples ask for clarification. Did they get it? Where else in Mark do the disciples go "in the house" with Jesus and what did they discuss?
- If you could go "in the house" with Jesus, what questions would you ask? What clarification would you want from Jesus?

**Proper 23/Ordinary Time28**
Job 23:1-9, 16-17; Hebrews 4:12-16; Mark 10:17-31

All three of the texts appointed for this Sunday involve seeing or being seen.

Job contended that God refused to be found. God hid, Job cried, and was unwilling to hear his complaint or heed his calls to be seen, heard, and acknowledged. Hebrews made the case that human beings could not handle being fully seen by God because God's word revealed intentions of the heart, thoughts unspoken. Nothing would be hidden from the God who judges us according not only to actions, but to mere intentions. Hence humanity's need for a High Priest, an intercessor, for Jesus Christ to make a case on our behalf, plead for mercy, and take on the punishment that should be our own. Mark told the story of the privileged person, the one with power and possessions, wealth and influence, who came to Jesus wanting an affirmation of all that he is and does, but gets truly seen, truly loved, yet unable to relinquish the image he has of himself for the sake of the one that reflected his Creator.

Job wanted a face-to-face meeting with God. Hebrews said we can't handle that kind of direct access to the divine. Jesus was looking the rich man straight in the eye and still he could not hear and heed the Word of the Lord. What does all of this mean for us when we feel that God has abandoned us, or we are in the midst of suffering wondering if the Spirit intercedes for us or we find ourselves on our knees in front of Jesus? Do we really want an audience with the Triune God or are we more like the rich man, seeking out God, yet unwilling to let God's gaze penetrate our worldly masks? The rich man met Jesus face to face, only to turn and walk in the opposite direction rather than give up his earthly security and status and follow Jesus. Often, we, like the rich man in Mark, have no idea what's good for us. We say we want eternal life, and yet we cling to that which sucks the life from us and others. We ask God a question, but we don't really want to hear the answer.

What strikes me the most about this story in Mark is the disciples' reaction to Jesus' declaration that those with wealth will have a tough time getting into the kingdom of God. The rich man was shocked and grieved. I can understand his response. All his life, his money had equaled access, favor, and special consideration. No doubt, he expected Jesus to affirm his piety and obedience to the commandments, give him a pat on the back, and send him on his way. The rich man perhaps thought: *I work hard. I got into a top-notch university. I volunteer with my church.* So, the rich man knelt before Jesus looking for yet one more seal of approval, one more accolade to add to the long list on his resume. But Jesus, loving him, asked that he stop acquiring — wealth, status, affirmation — and start relinquishing — power, money, privilege — in order to follow the One who didn't puff himself up, but poured himself out. The rich man wanted Jesus to confirm that he already had all the right answers. No wonder he was shocked and grieved as he left.

But why didn't the disciples understand that following Jesus meant giving up all that formerly held you captive? They would make their case a few verses later, noting all that they had left in order to be Jesus' disciples. Wouldn't they have imagined that this man must also lose his life to save it? Why were they so stunned that wealth was a barrier to discipleship?

The disciples seemed to think that if this commandment-following rich man didn't have an 'in' with God, who did? Were they equating money with God's favor? Did they think that riches and blessings were synonymous? Were they still failing to see the servant Lord right in front of them? I wonder if Jesus' statement burst their unvoiced thoughts and expectations that an earthly reward, money, power, or status would come through Jesus and this servanthood was a temporary path to a big payoff. I wonder if they, like many of us, secretly operated on the assumption that people get what they deserve.

But Jesus said it is easier for a camel to get through the eye of a needle than for someone who is rich to enter the kingdom of heaven. Jesus said many who are first will be last, and the last will be first. Jesus turned our way of operating upside down. Jesus flipped disciples' assumptions then and now. Poverty is not a divine judgment, punishment, or crime. Physical/monetary wealth is the problem. Without the power and grace of God, wealth could block the path to the kingdom of heaven. But seeing wealth as a problem? That's not how we operate.

It is telling that the commandments Jesus listed when questioned by the young man are those that dictate how God expects (and even requires) us to treat one another. Don't behave in ways that injure your fellow human beings. The rich man said, 'Right. I got it. I have not violated any of these. Followed them to the letter since my youth.' Worked hard. Got into a prestigious school. Volunteered at the soup kitchen. Check. Check. Check. But Jesus said you still need to sell your possessions and give your money to the poor and follow me. Following the commandments entails not just discreet acts or inaction, but your whole self. Following Jesus requires giving up participating in systems that oppress others, overturning them even when those systems benefit you. Following Jesus means seeing others, really seeing them when they are suffering often as a result of privilege you take for granted. Following Jesus calls us to see others and ourselves in ways we heretofore haven't or wouldn't or couldn't: as members of one body, hurting when any part of the body hurts, rejoicing with whatever part rejoices, inextricably united in Christ.

One wise person I know said, "You are only as happy as your least happy child." As Christians, we are only as happy, safe, secure as the least happy, safe, and secure member of the Body of Christ — or really, of God's beloved world. That's an entirely different way of seeing and being seen. It cuts through our thoughts and good intentions, revealing whether we want to be pious or we yearn to be faithful. We need Christ's intervention and intercession if we are to ever bring such vision to fruition. Thankfully, all things are possible for God. Just wait and see.

This week:

- When have you felt truly seen? When have you felt invisible? Have you ever felt as if God was hiding from you or that you were invisible to God?

- Do you ever think about God judging your thoughts and intentions? How does God's Word judge our thoughts and intentions?

- Hebrews instructs us to approach the throne of grace with boldness, and to find mercy and help in times of need. Do you think of prayer in that way? What does it mean to you that Jesus is our great high Priest?

- Why do you think Jesus says wealth makes it hard to enter the kingdom of God? What else did Jesus say were obstacles to entering the kingdom?

- The phrase "the first will be last and the last will be first" is found a number of places in the gospels. Where? What does it mean?

- If we are indeed one body in Christ, what is required of us when a part of the body is hurting?

Proper 24/Ordinary Time 29

Job 38:1-7 (34-41); Hebrews 5:1-10; Mark 10:35-45

I feel for Job this week.

We are on chapter 38 of the book of Job. Job has suffered much. In last week's readings, he finally took God to task and cried that God refused to hear his complaint and was silent in the face of his suffering. This week, God replied. Silent no more, God let Job have it in a breathless "who do you think you are?" diatribe. These verses have an "and another thing, Job" quality to them. Just when you think God was finished taking Job to task, God added another piece of evidence in the case against Job's audacity: "Where were you when I laid the foundations of the earth? Who determined its measurements — surely you know! Have the gates of death been revealed to you? 'Well, have they?!'"

God goes on for another entire chapter before Job responded. Even then, Job got three verses before God got going again for another chapter and a half. Clearly, if word count is any indication, Job didn't stand a chance in a debate with the Most High God. Neither, of course, do we. Neither, of course, does anyone. That's the point, right? All that we think we know, all our sure complaints, our certain righteousness, our well thought through plans and our confidence in God's will come to nothing in the face of God's power, majesty, wisdom, goodness, and grandeur. This is a text that tells us loud and clear that we are creatures and God is Creator and we'd do well not to forget this rock-bottom truth.

We so often do not know what we are asking for when we approach God. We think we know exactly what is best, what we need most, what God ought to do for and with us — forgetting that our ways are not God's ways, our thoughts not God's thoughts. James and John said to Jesus, "Teacher, we want you to do for us what we ask of you." Jesus honored their desire and asked in return, "What is it that you want me to do for you?" In one of the most honest confessions in scripture, they told Jesus exactly what they wanted: "Grant us to sit, one at your right hand and one at your left, in your glory." In other words, James and

John wanted status, power, proximity to a glory that would make them glorious, too. Let's give them points for transparency, I guess. Jesus, rather than going all: "Who do you think you are?" and: "Where were you when?" was utterly honest right back: "You have no idea what you are asking for, James and John. Are you able to drink of the cup I will drink, or be baptized with the baptism with which I am baptized?"

Then, in one of the most hubris-laden moments in scripture, James and John said, "We are able." The mind-blowing thing about this statement is that it comes right after Jesus had told them for the third time that he would suffer and die before being raised on the third day. Jesus said, "Well then, you will drink from that cup and be baptized with that baptism, but it isn't up to me who sits on my left or on my right." At this point, the other disciples tuned in and got mad. "Why do James and John get special status? What about us?" Once again, we human beings speak out of ignorance or pride or naivete. Once again, Jesus must set us straight.

We are asking the wrong questions - wanting the wrong things — capitulating to the wrong values — focused on the wrong priorities. Like God to Job, Jesus must confront the disciples, call them on their flawed thinking, and remind them of who God is and who they are in relationship to God and one another. If followers of Jesus seek to be great, then they must serve. Once again, we are told those who want to be first must be last. This message, this truth, this reality is not one James and John wanted to hear, nor did the other ten, nor do disciples through the ages, nor do we. We want Jesus to do for us what we ask of him — and when was the last time you asked Jesus to make you last of all? When was the last time you asked Jesus to make you a servant? When was the last time you heard a prayer in worship that said something like: "God, take away our status and our power, make us the least and the last." Can you imagine something like that as a tagline for the next stewardship campaign?

Sometimes I think about what might happen if we printed mission statements like that on our bulletins. Maybe, "First Presbyterian Church: Striving to be last." We are "first" church of wherever, after all. How about "Least Presbyterian Church"? We talk about servant leadership, but do we talk about being a servant? We often seek to serve, but rarely seek to be a servant.

We want Jesus to do for us what we ask, and rarely do we ask to be last. Rarely do we rejoice in being the least. Often, we want to tell God what to do or take God to task without recognizing that we have no idea what we are truly asking. Thankfully, God knows this about us and God loves us anyway. God, in fact, deals gently with us, through Jesus Christ.

When we do not know what we need or what we are asking God to do for us, when we don't know our proper place or recognize God's will, when we can't see past ourselves or our circumstances, when we think we know what is best but fail to seek what God says is better, Jesus interceded for us. In one of the most pastoral sentences in scripture we are told, "He is able to deal gently with the ignorant and wayward, since he himself was subject to weakness." We have a great High Priest who meets us in our ignorance and asks us with sincerity, "What is it that you want me to do for you?" And then does for us so much more than we can ever ask or imagine.

James and John wanted glory. Jesus offered salvation. James and John wanted status. Jesus offered relationship. James and John wanted power. Jesus offered purpose. James and John wanted greatness. Jesus offered life. James and John wanted recognition. Jesus offered grace. James and John wanted vindication. Jesus offered mercy. James and John, like gentiles then and now, wanted to lord it over others. Jesus offered them, and us, the privilege of serving side by side, with him. We want to be first, but Jesus reminds us that we are closest to him when we are among the least and last and lost.

Thanks be to God, no matter what we ask, we have a great High Priest who intercedes for us, and through his death and resurrection, has already given us all we could ever need.

This week:

- How do you feel when you read these verses from Job? Is it fair that God takes Job to task given all that Job has endured?

- What have you asked of Jesus? Did you receive it?
- What do we make of the juxtaposition of James' and John's request with Jesus' admonishment elsewhere "to ask and receive"?
- What would it look like for churches or individual Christians to be "last" or "least" or "servants of all"?
- Who do you relate to in this story from Mark? Do you see yourself as James or John? The other ten? When have you gotten angry that someone else had gotten something you thought they didn't deserve or that you may have wanted?
- When you pray, do you consider the promise that Christ intercedes for you? Prays for us? As you pray this week, be aware of this truth and note what difference it makes in your praying.

## Proper 25/Ordinary Time 30
### Job 42:1-6, 10-17; Hebrews 7:23-28; Mark 10:46-52

I found myself getting emotional as I read and studied the texts appointed for this fall Sunday.

Job, humbled, confessed to God: "I uttered what I did not understand, things too wonderful for me. I despise myself and repent in dust and ashes." In an age when humility is out of fashion and a time when, according to Jonathan Merritt in a recent New York Times article, words like "love," "patience," "gentleness" and "faithfulness" are "much rarer," Job's confession strikes a countercultural chord. Merritt sited a study in The Journal of Positive Psychology that revealed that the use of "humility words, like 'modesty,' fell by 53 %." Even people of faith resist repenting in dust in ashes, save for Ash Wednesday. Rarely do we acknowledge our ignorance, even when it comes to the mind of God. Job's broken and contrite heart nonetheless resonates with those of us who have known despair, loss, and the dark night of the soul. There is a freeing honesty about his raw confession.

Job hit a spiritual rock bottom familiar to anyone who has struggled with deep sorrow, extended suffering, or acute guilt. In the depths of darkness, our anger spent, our limitations laid bare, we turn to God, plead for mercy and wait. The patience of Job, indeed.

Hebrews reminds us, however, that we do not wait or plead or cry alone. Jesus, the permanent High Priest, intercedes for us. The beautiful, breathtaking promise given us is this: Jesus "is able for all time to save those who approach God through him." We may sit in dust and ashes for a season, but through the One who lives always to make intercession for us, our cries are met with the word to take heart because we've been heard. We will not be left to wallow in the dust, muck, or ash forever.

Jesus heard Bartimaeus. Jesus called for him. Jesus asked him: "What do you want me to do for you?" Jesus offered the dignity of asking someone long sidelined and silenced to speak for himself, to have his voice heard, honored, and tended. Jesus, the Messiah, the Son of David, refused to assume he knew what was best for Bartimaeus. When countless people sternly ordered Bartimaeus to be quiet, not make a scene, not to disrupt, to accept his fate, Jesus stopped, called for him, and asked him: "What do you want?" Jesus listened and gave Bartimaeus that for which he asked, requiring nothing in return. Jesus told him, "Go, your faith has made you well." Bartimaeus instead followed on the way. Imagine if Jesus' disciples, the church, Christ's body, responded likewise to the marginalized, silenced, suffering, and vulnerable? Imagine if our prayers and practices imitated those of the great High Priest, the Son of David, our Lord?

What if we sought to bring not just words like "love," "patience," "gentleness," and "faithfulness" back into the cultural lexicon, but back into our daily practices? Jesus' exchange with Bartimaeus, son of Timaeus, gave us a model for doing just that.

First, the "blind beggar" had a name, a family, a place. He was Bartimaeus, son of Timaeus who lived in Jericho.

Driving with my husband recently there was a man sitting at the end of the interstate exit ramp with a cardboard sign asking for help. My husband said, "Oh, that's Paul." I looked at him, surprised he knew the man's name. My husband continued: "Sometimes I see him near my office. We've talked. He has diabetes and we've exchanged stories on the difficulty of eating right and keeping it in check." We pulled up to the stop sign, my husband leaned out the window and said: "Paul! How are you?"

Every "blind beggar" has a name, a family, a story, a place. Gentleness, faithfulness, love, and patience call us to know people by name, not by condition or circumstance.

Second, when someone cries out for help, at the very least, we ought not order them to be silent. Disciples of Jesus Christ must honor the pain and hurt of those made in God's image. Some of us, myself too often included, value politeness and civility over justice. I confess to being guilty of bowing down to the golden calf of decency and order. Those exploited, abused, neglected, and hurting should cry out and be heard. God desires abundant life for all people, not a false peace for those with the ability to cross to the other side of the street.

Third, Jesus stopped. That adage that "ministry is the interruptions" rings true in this text. Jesus, time after time, even on the way to Jerusalem, stopped when someone cried out to him, touched him, or asked him for help. Do we? How often have we refused to hear and heed the cries of Bartimaeus because we've been too busy doing the work of the Lord? When anyone musters up the courage to call out, to come forward, to say, "Do you have a minute?" our faithful, Christ-like response is to stop and see and hear and attend to him.

Fourth, Jesus asked Bartimaeus what he wanted. Jesus did not presume to know the needs, longings, and hopes of the one who was in front of him. Good-intentioned church people often presume to know what other people need. We collect clothing and send it to disaster zones when what would truly be helpful is a check. We go on a mission trip, and our own need to "do something" imposes a project on a community that might really need and want our willingness to listen and learn how we could be in relationship for the long haul. Do we ask what others want and need, or do we presume to know best?

Finally, Jesus gave Bartimaeus that for which he asked with nothing required in return. This was no transaction, no quid pro quo. There was no gratitude or deference expected. Jesus freely gave, Bartimaeus was free to respond as he was moved. Jesus said, "Go." Bartimaeus chose to follow Jesus on the way. Would that our mission, evangelism, and discipleship were equally as gracious, generous, and unencumbered. Would that we, like Job, recognize the extent of our limited understanding and confess it, knowing that Jesus interceded for us, heard and heeds our cries, and grants us the privilege of hearing and heeding the cries of others in his name.

Those of us who've known the mercy, grace, gentleness, and patience of the great High Priest, who've been seen and heard, honored and healed, saved and redeemed by Jesus Christ, yearn to follow on the way and do likewise. Such grace is beyond our understanding, too wonderful for us, and yet, through Jesus Christ, we know it to be true.

This week:

- Have you ever presumed to know what someone else needed? Has someone ever presumed to know what you needed?

- When have you realized that you "uttered what you did not understand"? Have you ever despised yourself? Were you able to confess, repent, and receive God's forgiveness?

- Pay attention to conversations you hear and have this week. Do you notice "spiritual" or "religious" language? Do you notice acts that reflect that language: gentleness, patience, love, and so on?

- Take time this week to get to know someone's name and maybe even part of her story. Really see and hear someone you may not have previously seen or heard.

- How have you sternly ordered someone to be quiet? Have you ever been told to be silent when you have been crying out for help or justice?

- Be mindful as you pray and work, rest and play, that Jesus Christ "always lives to make intercession" for you. Remember that Christ right now prays for you.

Proper 26/Ordinary Time 31
Ruth 1:1-18; Hebrews 9:11-14; Mark 12:28-34

At first reading of the gospel text this week, I marveled at the audacity of the scribe in Mark's version of this story.

The scribe said to Jesus, "You are right, teacher." The scribe felt he had the authority to affirm Jesus' response. The scribe graded Jesus, the teacher. I marveled too at Jesus' response to the scribe's presumptuous confirmation of his answer. Jesus told this scribe, "You are not far from the kingdom of God." Jesus did not say, "Of course I am right!" or "Who do you think you are assessing my answer?' Jesus saw that this scribe understood the bottom-line bulwark of the faith: love God and neighbor. And therefore Jesus said, "You are not far from the kingdom of God."

This affirmation of the scribe is particularly striking, as it is the only time in Mark's gospel where a scribe gets a shout-out from Jesus. This exchange was no pleasant, churchy small talk. This back-and-forth between Jesus and one of the scribes represented a radical new possibility of relationship, understanding, and religion. Even scribes who had done all they could to test, trap, and destroy Jesus could be moved by that very Jesus to a different understanding of religion and a new relationship with God and neighbor. In Mark's version of this story Jesus quoted the Shema, "Hear, O Israel: the Lord our God, the Lord is one." Everything else flows from this reality of the one and only God. This scribe knew this affirmation better than anyone and proclaimed that from this truth came love directed to God and toward neighbor. This truth rendered even religious ritual secondary. The scribe, the keeper, and arbitrator of those rituals, recognized their limits and their penultimate position to love of the one God and all neighbors.

No wonder Jesus said to this scribe, "You are not far from the kingdom of God." This scribe experienced an epiphany and Jesus recognized the transformation. The scribe had eyes to see and ears to hear. Perhaps his response to Jesus's answer wasn't so much presumptuous as it was an enthusiastic "ah-ha," eureka-type moment. Maybe this scribe was "amening" the Word of God he just heard, and Jesus was confirming his faithful response to the Word of the Lord.

This exchange was not about either Jesus or the scribe getting the right answer on the Bible content exam. This exchange was a conversion. The scribe's affirmation was worship, an affirmation of faith. All the scribe thought he understood, he saw differently and now knew by heart, moving him closer to the kingdom of God.

Have you ever had such a revelation? I recently preached a sermon on a text I'd preached many times before. Part of the text had been read at my wedding. It was a passage I loved, returned to regularly, prayed, studied, and taught. It was Colossians 3:1-17, the poetic verses on living as a new self, the new self in Christ. It contains the parenetic phrase "but now" that tips the reader off to the list of ways we should now be living, given that we've learned by heart the command to love God and neighbor. You know that "you were once" all these ugly, evil things, but now you are gentle, patient, humble, loving, and kind. For years I preached and taught that we should be striving harder to make our lives match all that came after the "but now." The problem being, of course, that no matter how hard I tried, a lot of my life reflected the "you were once." It felt like the makeover didn't stick and I wondered what was wrong with me. (Okay — and what was wrong with other Christians, too.)

However, over the course of writing the sermon on this text this time I had an "ah-ha," forehead-slapping moment. Like the scribe in Mark I said to Jesus, "You are right, teacher!" I realized that the "but now" isn't my perfect behavior, but rather Jesus' perfect love and sacrifice that frees me to be who and whose I truly am. The "but now" is the life, death and resurrection of Jesus Christ, not my flawless discipleship. I am clothed in Christ even when my outward appearance doesn't much imitate him.

I had the focus all wrong all these years. Like Jesus in Mark's gospel, I should have started with "Hear, O Israel: the Lord our God, the Lord is one." Our lives should always, first and foremost, be directed toward the Lord our God, the one and only God. We are to worship our Lord, love him with all our heart, soul, mind, and strength. From there comes our love of neighbor as ourselves, wanting for them what we want for ourselves, working for their wellbeing as we seek our own, caring for them as we care for our own flesh and blood. That's how we get closer to the kingdom of God. Those rituals and sacrifices, our morality and good behavior, these are important, but they won't grant us entrance to the kingdom. Only the life, love, and sacrifice of Jesus Christ that reconciles us to God and each other. "You are right, teacher!"

The writer of Hebrews understood this truth. "For if the blood of goats and bulls, with the sprinkling of the ashes of a heifer, sanctifies those who have been defiled so that their flesh is purified, how much more will the blood of Christ, who through the eternal Spirit offered himself without blemish to God, purify our conscience from dead works to worship the living God!"

The passage from Mark ended with silence. No one dared ask another question. We are left to wonder if the scribe followed Jesus as a result of this scales-removed-from-his-eyes experience. Like other parts of Mark's gospel, readers are invited to fill in the silence with their own stories. If we know that Jesus is right — that God is one and that the greatest commandment is to love God with all we've got and our neighbors as ourselves — will we follow Jesus and try our best to do so, trusting that when we fail (and we will fail), Christ the High Priest with his own blood has obtained our eternal redemption. Once we know Jesus, our teacher, is right, what will we do with that knowledge that is now written on our hearts?

This week:

- When have you had a revelation where you saw something in a brand new way? When have you had an epiphany?
- When Jesus said to the scribe, "You are not far from the kingdom of God," was he implying that the scribe wasn't quite there yet? Or was he acknowledging how far the scribe had come in his understanding of God?

- When you think about loving God with all your heart, soul, mind, and strength, what does that look like? Are their distinct ways we love God with our heart? Soul? Mind? Strength?
- How do we love our neighbor "as ourselves"? What does that "as" mean to you?
- Why do you think the scribes dared not ask Jesus another question? Why did Jesus' response silence them?
- What is the relationship between the three objects of love in this passage: God, neighbor, and self?

## All Saints' Day
Isaiah 25:6-9; Revelation 21:1-6a; John 11:32-44

I didn't watch the video. I didn't want to see. Hearing was difficult enough.

The BBC reporter in his detached newscaster voice shared the dying six-year-old Yemini boy's plea to the doctors working on his body, his small body badly injured by a missile that had struck his house. The boy, in tears, said, "Don't bury me." A reporter shared the footage of Fareed's last words on his Facebook page and after the little boy died it went viral. The story on the BBC website is titled, "A dying boy's plea that became an iconic message for peace." The BBC reports that a Yemini activist posted on Facebook, "Just like young Aylan (Kurdis) death encapsulated the tragedy of the Syrian people, Fareed's plea not to be buried encapsulates the tragedy of the Yemini people." (https://www.bbc.com/news/blogs-trending-34572137)

I am embarrassed to admit that I had to Google "conflict in Yemen" to be reminded of who was fighting whom and why. Syria had been on my mind and in my prayers, but not Yemen. In recent days, I have been trying to both keep in mind and push from my consciousness the photos in Time magazine's special report, "Exodus." The images are black and white, featuring young men and old women, children carried on their parents' shoulders and trudging along behind them, all of them with looks of painful determination on their faces. The report offers daunting statistics like, "If this population were a country, it would be the world's 24th largest." "Half of all refugees are children." I want to hold these realities close. I want to forget them completely.

Then I hear of a little boy, begging the adults surrounding him, "Don't bury me" and I feel accountable. I feel compelled to remember Aylan and Fareed on this All Saints' Day. This November 1, as I remember my beloved father-in-law who died way too soon and my grandparents and church members I have buried and miss, I also feel a need to remember those in the communion of the saints I don't know but dare not forget.

The texts for this week in Isaiah and in Revelation are about community on the grandest scale. They are about God's long awaited redemption of whole peoples, of the entire creation, a new heaven and a new earth, after all. Listen to the scope of this redemption in Isaiah:

"On this mountain the Lord of hosts will make for all peoples a feast of rich food, a feast of well-aged wines… and he will destroy on this mountain the shroud that is cast over all peoples, the sheet that is spread over all nations; he will swallow up death forever."

Hear the intimacy of this relationship in Revelation: "See, the home of God is among mortals. He will dwell with them as their God; they will be his peoples, and God himself will be with them; he will wipe every tear from their eyes. Death will be no more; mourning and crying and pain will be no more, for the first things have passed away."

There is both a powerful expansiveness and a tender closeness in these texts that call on us to lift up both God's majesty and God's immediacy for us and for all people. This is *All* Saints' Day. God hasn't forgotten Aylan or Fareed. Nor has God neglected the ones you have loved and missed, the saints in the cemetery behind the church or the ones interred in the columbarium beside it. We need to remember them all.

Don't bury them. Don't imagine that death has the last word, either. Too often resurrection is left to Easter Sunday; we don't even observe the entire season. It is as if we can only suspend our disbelief in the finality of death for a few hours, once a year. We sing "Alleluia," and then live as if Jesus never left the tomb, relegating the tragedies of our time to the category of inevitable, insurmountable, and beyond hope. We ignore the pleas of Fareed. We allow the rhythms of the news cycle to focus and frame our attention even as vast numbers of people continue to suffer long after the cameras are turned off. We recite the correct faith statement, "I know that he will rise again in the resurrection on the last day… I believe that you are the Messiah, the Son of God, the one coming into the world." But we fail to act on that belief, ignoring Jesus' command to move the stone. We neglect to unbind the ones Jesus has called forth from the grave.

All Saints' Day is a day to preach resurrection, to have the audacity to proclaim that death, destruction, violence, and pain aren't ultimate. All three of these texts for All Saints' Day are about God's ability and certain promise to bring about long awaited and seemingly impossible reconciliation, redemption, and life. The question we have to ask ourselves and those gathered is: Do you believe this?

This is a Sunday to invite people to dare to believe in what much of the world says is impossible and then ask them to live in ways that reflect that radical belief: God hears and heeds the pleas of all of his children crying, "Don't bury me." God's home is among mortals. God destroys the shrouds that have been cast over all peoples. The Lord wipes away the tears of Fareed and all faces. God is creating a new heaven and a new earth. Death and mourning and crying will be no more. Do you believe this?

Remember *all* the saints this Sunday, hear the cries of the vulnerable, look at the haunting photos, grieve for the suffering in the world and the sadness in the room. But do not grieve as those without hope, instead grieve as those who expect to see the glory of God. Don't forget we are followers of the God of resurrection, the ones who go down to the grave singing alleluia, alleluia, alleluia. Trusting in the truth that through Christ death has been and will be defeated, we can get to work, rolling away grave stones and unbinding those Jesus has brought back to life, no matter how many there are, no matter how many days have past.

This week:

- One commentator wrote, "John's gospel begins with a wedding and ends with a funeral." (Social Science Commentary on the *Gospel of John* Crossmarks.com) What do you think the significance of this is?
- Read John chapter 11 in its entirety. Note the similarities and differences in Martha and Mary's response to Jesus. Pay attention to how Jesus' giving of life led to the call for Jesus' death.

- This story in John revealed an emotional Jesus. Jesus was deeply moved, he wept, he was disturbed. Are there other gospel stories where Jesus was described in this way? Are we comfortable with this level of emotion in Jesus?
- Is there a danger in holding up these promises of no more suffering when people are suffering? How are texts like these helpful to those in the midst of profound loss? How are they potentially problematic?
- Where in the world is experiencing violence and how can you help?
- Pray for those mentioned the headlines this week, countries and people alike.

## Proper 27/Ordinary Time 32
Ruth 3:1-5; 4:13-17; Hebrews 9:24-28; Mark 12:38-44

What obligation do we have to those in our society who cannot provide for themselves? What responsibility do those who follow the Triune God have for people that are systemically oppressed, marginalized, and vulnerable?

The texts appointed for this week will not let us dodge these basic questions of what it means to be faithful to the God who came to bring good news to the poor and let the oppressed go free. While our country roils with conflict, division, violence, vitriolic rhetoric and deadly acts, the Bible holds us accountable to how we treat the disinherited. Jesus takes sides and tells us with whom we are to stand if we want to be with him. The scriptures require us to examine our hearts, actions, and witness in the face of our current context and every shocking headline. Begin with how we treat the least of these, the systemically oppressed and the situationally vulnerable, no matter who they are.

How do we treat the widows in our day? Naomi knows all too well that without a man to protect them, she and Ruth risk destitution and death. Naomi said to her daughter-in-law, "I need to seek some security for you." That security was Boaz, the next of kin; and as it turns out, he was a moral and good man. Naomi gave Ruth explicit instructions that almost sounded like advice from a 1950s women's magazine: Clean yourself up and make yourself look good — and go get close to Boaz. "He will tell you what to do."

Boaz followed the religious rules. He made sure a closer next of kin did not want to be Ruth's husband's. He sent Ruth home with six measures of barley and eventually took Ruth as his wife. She bore a son, Obed, father of Jesse, father of David. Naomi and Ruth's story moved forward and that of Israel, too. A disastrous, tragic ending was avoided due to the goodness of Boaz.

While not exactly a resounding win for feminism, Boaz acted righteously and within the customs and constrictions of the time.

He demonstrated proper care for widows, the most vulnerable of the vulnerable.

Contrast this story of Boaz with that of the scribes in Mark's gospel. Jesus called them out for their showy piety, devoid of care for the widows. Worse, they not only failed to provide for the weak and marginalized but they exploited them, the very ones they were called to care for and protect. More than praising the widow for giving all she had to the temple, Jesus condemned the temple economy that demanded that even those who had nothing should give everything.

Making this a stewardship text about sacrificial giving gets too many of us off the hook for holding institutions, church, and otherwise, accountable for systemic oppression of the already marginalized. Think of cash bail, payday loans, and court fines that keep escalating. The widow putting in her very last coin was akin to refugees and migrants paying smugglers as they flee for their lives. The widow should not have been giving all she had to the temple treasury. The scribes of the temple should have been giving from that treasury to care for the widow.

Ched Myers, in his book *Binding the Strong Man*, put it thusly: "The temple has robbed this woman of her very means of livelihood. Like the scribal class, it no longer protects widows, but exploits them. As if in disgust, Jesus 'exits' the temple — for the last time."

Over and over again, the litmus test which represents our loyalty to our God, our faithfulness to Jesus Christ, and the obedience to the Lord is determined through this: How do we treat the poor and vulnerable? Do we care for the least of these?

Over and over again, God's prophets and God's Son reserve the harshest judgment for those who profess belief in God all the while exploiting, oppressing and hurting those already suffering. Scribes, Pharisees, unjust judges, woe to those who do not extend compassion, mercy, tangible care, and protection to widows and orphans.

The call of Jesus is unambiguous: Do not exploit the vulnerable. Care for those the world relentlessly seeks to crush.

The judgment of God is explicit: Woe to you who tithe mint and rue and herbs of all kinds, but neglect justice and love of God (Luke 11:42-

43). You shall not abuse any widow or orphan. If you do abuse them, when they cry out to me, I will surely heed their cry; my wrath will burn, and I will kill you with the sword, and your wives shall become widows and your children orphans (Exodus 22:22-24).

Any questions?

Howard Thurman, in *Jesus and the Disinherited* wrote: "Too often the price exacted by society for security and respectability is that the Christian movement in its formal expression must be on the side of the strong against the weak. This is a matter of great significance, for it reveals to what extent a religion that was born of a people acquainted with persecution and suffering has become the cornerstone of a civilization and of nations whose very position in modern life has too often been secured by a ruthless use of power applied to weak and defenseless peoples."

Too often Christians have sold their soul for the sake of some perceived sense of personal security with the widow paying the price for their "safety" with her last coin, with her very life.

*Presbyterian Outlook* reporter Leslie Scanlon recently went to the border between Mexico and the United States to see firsthand what was happening to migrants and asylum seekers there. Her stories reveal both heartbreaking suffering and heartening acts of compassion. Reporting from the shelter, La Posada Providencia, Scanlon interviewed the executive director Andi Atkinson: "An asylum seeker is 'someone who had to leave their country, but didn't want to leave their country — kind of like Mary and Joseph,' she said. 'It's kind of amazing how many Americans don't want to let in immigrants any more, especially if those immigrants are poor and people of color. It's amazing how many Christians don't want to let immigrants in, even though the gospel mandates you are supposed to treat the foreign-born the same as the natives. So many Christians have forgotten some basic things from the Bible." https://pres-outlook.org/tag/on-the-border/

This week's reading puts front and center, in plain sight, some basic things from the Bible, some basic instructions and admonishments from Jesus: Do not abuse, exploit, or neglect the vulnerable. Care for widows and orphans. Woe to you religious leaders who use your positions and power for your own gain and at the expense of others.

Any questions?

This week:

- Use a Bible concordance and look up the words "widow" and "orphan." What do you discover?
- Read all of the verses between those appointed in Ruth for this week. What do these additional verses reveal about Boaz?
- Who are the most vulnerable people in your church? Community? Our world? How are we caring for them?
- How are "widows and orphans" being exploited in our time? How do we combat that exploitation?
- Is it a misreading of this text from Mark to use it as a call to sacrificial giving? Why or why not?
- Look at the parallel texts to the Markan one for this week in Luke 20:45-47 and Matthew 23:1-36. How do these accounts inform the one from Markan?

## Proper 28/ Ordinary Time 33
1 Samuel 1:4-20; Hebrews 10:11-14 (15-18) 19-25; Mark 13:1-8

Occasionally, when the "Presbyterian Outlook" staff emails one another, we begin with "Today's Sign of the End Times," and follow it with an unexpected and strange request, response, or article.

This churchy humor helps us weather the ups and downs of being on the receiving end of many public comments and frequent scrutiny, some of it is kind, some of it not so kind, some of it is downright odd. But when I come to chapter thirteen of Mark's gospel, I realize that our "signs of the end times" are not Jesus' signs of the end times. Jesus' signs do not call forth eye rolls, laughter, a chuckle, or stress relief. Jesus' talk of the end times arrests us and causes us to question expectations and events roiling all around us.

Jesus tells his disciples who marvel at the beautiful, imposing temple (that same temple and scribal system he has been railing against) that even an institution and edifice that big, that established, and that powerful will not stand forever. "All will be thrown down." All. What did Jesus include in that "all"? The temple, yes. But everything else, too? Governments? Palaces? Military forts? Impressive corporate headquarters and historic landmarks? Will all be thrown down? Why? When? How? To what end? What remains? What comes next? Like the disciples who pulled Jesus aside in Mark's gospel, I too have a lot of questions about the predicted end times.

Peter, James, John, and Andrew asked Jesus: "When will this be? How will we know this is accomplished?" Jesus then began his sermon with a warning: Don't go astray. Don't believe messianic impersonators.

Anticipating the disciples' ability throughout time to ascribe to Jesus beliefs and ideas antithetical to the gospel, Jesus warned: Don't be lead astray. Then he went straight to the scary and apocalyptic. He calmly laid out the certain upheaval to come: wars, civil wars, natural disasters, famine. But don't be alarmed, He admonished.

Wars, civil wars, natural disasters, famine. Check, check, check and check. I can read the headlines and spin the globe on any given day and see Jesus' signs of the end times emblazed in print or pixels. I confess, I am alarmed. Even if these are the birth pangs of the new life, new era, new God-thing on the horizon, I am alarmed. I have no idea if these are signs of the end times. We Christians have been waiting a long time. We've been in labor for millennia with no pain relief in sight. All has not been thrown down. The world order of the rich getting richer and the poor getting trampled remains. Have you seen that bumper sticker? "If you aren't outraged, you aren't paying attention." How, Jesus, can we not be alarmed?

The recent climate report that detailed how we are about to fall off a global warming cliff alarms me. The images of starving children in Yemen, babies of skin and bones, alarms me. Reading stories of people risking their lives, leaving all they have, walking to our border in order to escape poverty and violence and terror, alarms me. Another mass shooting — and another — and another. I am nothing but alarmed right now and this promise of a birth somewhere in the sometime future does not assuage my ever-growing anxiety. Women, after all, die in childbirth with *alarming* frequency. Jesus, how can you tell your followers, "do not be alarmed"?

Is it faithful enough to not be utterly paralyzed? If we cannot keep calm and carry on, is it acceptable in your sight, Jesus, to gird our loins and enter the chaos in your name? Can we be alarmed, scared as hell, and persevere, using our provocation to provoke one another to love and perform good deeds? Would that be an adequate and faithful response to all that alarms us? I might be able to muster that courage, with your help.

But first, I need to stop in the temple while it still stands and pray like a drunkard alongside Hannah. I need to beg for new life, for hope, for relief. I need a reassuring word from Jesus, yes, but also from Eli, from a fellow believer with more perspective and a little more confidence that you will do what you promise. I don't care how foolish, crazed, or uncollected I appear. I am feeling foolish, crazed, and uncollected. I need to pour out my heart to you for a while, lament those crushed by poverty, drowned in the natural disasters, left to die in deserts, dance floors, and war zones. Do you hear, Lord? Eli? Can we talk in private, because I have some questions about the similarities between the end times and our times, and I'd like a few answers, please. I am a woman who is deeply troubled and I know I am not alone in that sentiment right now.

I need not only to pray to God and hear from a caring and competent religious leader, I need the other members of the household of God, too. Could we meet together and talk about this? Can we comfort one another and cry together and share some signs of hope while we are at it? Could we help each other hold fast to that which is good and render no one evil for evil? Could you spur me to love and good deeds and I'll do the same for you?

I do not know what time it is. What I do know is this: Many are perishing. Wars rage on for generations. God's good people and God's good creation are in peril. I am alarmed. But Jesus assures me of his presence, his power, his will to reconcile, redeem, save, and make whole. Jesus has given us himself and he has given us one another. Whatever time it is, we are not at the end. That means we hope. That means we need to meet together. That means we pray. That means we provoke one another to love and good deeds. That means we stay with the pain, breathe, and hold fast to the one who gives us a Son who never turns away from the hurt of the world. That means we relentlessly work for peace no matter how persistent the violence, we help those in the middle of disasters, natural or otherwise, we feed the hungry and care for the sick, knowing that's how we want to be found whenever Jesus returns and whenever our end, or the end, comes.

This week:

- Do you ever think about the end times? What does it mean to you? How is your life shaped by Jesus' Words in this week's gospel reading?
- Are you alarmed? If so, why? Is being alarmed unfaithful?

- The Hebrews text admonishes Christians to meet together. How are you meeting together and what difference do those gatherings make for you? Others?
- How do we provoke one another to love and good deeds?
- Have you ever prayed like Hannah? Was there an Eli present to hear and counsel you?
- Have you ever been in the presence of one who was deeply troubled? How did you respond?

The language of "king" perplexes and confounds.

For some, it creates a stumbling block to seeing God: male, dominating, subjugating, and hierarchical. These are adjectives akin to anathema in our postmodern, #MeToo, pluralistic culture, right? Hard as I try, that scene from "Monty Python and the Holy Grail" keeps playing in my head:

"I am your king."

"Well, I didn't vote for you."

"You don't vote for kings."

We, too, question kingship: Who made you king? Who gives you authority? How will that authority be enforced? Over what do you have authority, anyway? I didn't vote for you.

Given our tendency to chafe at such regal expressions of power, what do we do with Christ the King Sunday? How do we wrestle with such authority in our cultural season of anti-institutionalism and conspiracy theories? How do we talk about obedience, or fear of the Lord, or reign of God, or the King of kings? The three texts appointed for this week give good clues for where to start. Samuel 2 offers a window into the role and character God requires of earthly leaders. Revelation gives a beautiful glimpse into the glorious, majestic, all-encompassing power of the risen Christ. John makes sure we never forget that the one we worship, the Lord of all, poured himself out to the point of death on a cross. Christ the King is no dictator, despot or tyrant. None of those adjectival anathemas apply to Jesus Christ.

Those of us who worship Jesus Christ place ourselves in his service and seek to follow, beginning with the recognition that we are not to lord it over others. Our witness is counter to the prevailing and perennial example of worldly leaders who abuse their positions by exploiting the ones for whom they are charged to care. Jesus, our teacher and master, washed feet. He told us to do likewise. If the Spirit of the Lord speaks through us, our words and acts reflect the God who calls us. To rule justly is to fear God and no other. Christ the King Sunday demands that we assess how we use our influence and power, our privilege and gifts. Do we lord it over others or instead seek their interest? Do we look to please God or capitulate to earthly adulation? Do we strive for integrity or scramble for status? Christ the King is the servant Lord and our lives should imitate his example.

Christ the King, the risen Christ, "the faithful witness, the firstborn of the dead, and the ruler of the kings of the earth" is the one "who loves us and freed us from our sins by his blood, and made us to be a kingdom, priests serving his God and Father." The One now seated at the right hand of God to judge the quick and the dead, made us to be a kingdom of priests who worship God and care for the people and in so doing serve the Lord. Even in glory, the King of kings intercedes for us, prays for us, never abandons us. Until that time when we gather around the heavenly throne, we can be encouraged because we are not alone, nor are we without purpose. The risen Christ enlists us into service for the sake of the world he so loves. We are made regents, entrusted to act in the name of Jesus Christ. Such knowledge ought to give us pause, humble us and move us to prayer. Executive orders and unilateral decrees are not the stock and trade of Christians. We work together in community (and yes, on committee) — one body with many members, with Christ and no other at the head. The will we seek to discern is Christ's, regardless of what other authorities may want.

Jesus Christ, our Savior, the very one betrayed, arrested, beaten, mocked, and summoned by Pilate, who told the ruler with the power to kill him: "My kingdom is not from this world." Faced with the opportunity to spare himself, he chose truth over safety. Jesus said he came to testify to the truth. Whoever belongs to that truth listens to his voice. Are we listening to Jesus' voice? In a season awash in lies, a time when not just talk, but truth is deemed cheap or worthless, those of us who worship the king of the Jews must testify to the truth, no matter the cost. In the words of Katie Cannon, Women in Ministry Conference,: "Even when they tell you your truth is a lie. Tell it anyway."

When earthly kings, prefects, emperors, and politicians shrug their shoulders and ask dismissively, "What is truth?", the disciples of Jesus bear witness to the truth. God's truth, the gospel truth. The eternal, unchanging truth of the Ten Commandments, the prophets, the Sermon on the Mount, Jesus' new commandment and his words from the cross. No matter the cost. No matter how many refuse to hear it. No matter if some seek to silence it. No matter if people in positions of power, secular and religious, condemn it and us.

The language of kingship may gall or grate, but only if we equate our king with earthly authorities. Like so many other words, concepts and institutions, the model of Jesus reframes, redefines, reforms, and restores this one. On Christ the King Sunday, point to Jesus: risen Lord, servant Savior, crucified Messiah. Point to Christ the King of kings in all you do and say. Fear God. Strive for God's will and not your own. Be the priestly regents who extend forgiveness and compassion in the name of the one who anoints and appoints us. Never forget that the body of which we are a part has the head of Jesus who wore a crown of thorns. Testify to that truth. The gospel truth. God's truth. The truth the world needs to know.

This week:

- Do you struggle with the language of "king" and "kingdom?" Why or why not? Are there other words you might use or choose?

- Some use the word "kin-dom" to describe Christian community. Do you find this helpful? What is gained and what is lost when we use "kin-dom" rather than "kingdom?"

- What does it mean to testify to the truth? What do you think Jesus means by this? What does this mean for disciples?

- What are your spheres of influence? Where do you have authority, power, or sway? How are you using it? Does your use of power reflect and further the gospel?

- How do you listen to Jesus' voice? What do you hear when you listen to Jesus' voice?

- What difference does it make that Jesus is the "King of kings" or the "ruler of the kings of the earth?"

## Thanksgiving Day
Joel 2:2-27; I Timothy 2:1-7; Matthew 6:25-33

I don't much like Thanksgiving. What's not to like? There are the three F's — food, family, and football, not necessarily in that order. I like those three F's. I do. Even so, I struggle every year. For a long time, I felt a vague sense of dread with no ability to name what about Thanksgiving left me feeling bereft. Then I realized that this is a holiday without a direct tie to Jesus. The day isn't on every liturgical calendar; it is always on the secular one, and that's okay, but it leaves me without an anchor to hold me fast. Without a greater theological cord to which I can be tied, I tend to buy what American culture sells. That's when I begin to think I am lacking. That's when I notice that my family doesn't match the one depicted in the billboards, commercials, and magazines. That's when I think I had better get shopping for Christmas before dawn the next day.

Don't get me wrong, I have a great family, but my family is more like Waffle House hash browns — smothered, covered, chunked, and diced — than Grandma's ever present, been-in-the-family-for-years-recipe for pumpkin pie. My brother and his husband are in Boston. My dad and his wife live in Alabama. My husband's dad died twenty years ago. My mom and stepfather are in North Carolina and my mother-in-law and her new (ish) husband in North Carolina, too. My sister will be with her husband's family. My husband's sister lives in China.

The doorbell won't ring repeatedly with loved ones coming from near and far bringing heaping plates of food. A few of us will gather, some combination of the above list of people I love, but who don't necessarily all love each other. We will eat well. We will be polite because the years when we haven't been kind to each other hang in the air like the aroma of the roasting bird, if not nearly so pleasant. We won't go around the table and each say what we are thankful for, because our family just can't pull off such an expressive ritual with authenticity. Holding hands for the blessing maxes out our outward show of emotion for the day.

Truth be told, most of us would rather be reading — in the same room is fine, but undisturbed by conversation.

None of this matches the Norman Rockwell painting or the Publix ad or the spreads in "Southern Living". And without Jesus to remind me of what truly matters, I start to imagine that my family — scattered, divorced, remarried, unsentimental, introverted — doesn't measure up, isn't enough, or that it should be somehow other than what it is. That's why I don't much like the day on which I am to be the most thankful. I need an explicit connection to Jesus: incarnation, repentance, redemption, resurrection, even crucifixion. That way, I'll know where to look for God when the tattered ends of relationships start to show and expectations aren't fully met and world views clash. I need Jesus to be the true north on the compass to help me navigate my way through the meal and the day and the weekend.

So, this year I am going to be sure to invite him. If I invite Jesus, I am certain he will come. He likes to go to people's homes for dinner. He doesn't require polite company. He seems unfazed by tableside drama. Even a woman weeping on his feet was welcomed, so perhaps my family can somehow be holy, too. We aren't the perfect family. We've been known to hurt each other. Seasons of estrangement have come and gone. We won't all be in the same room at the same time this Thanksgiving, but regardless we will be united in Christ, held together by the One who not only ate with sinners, but came to save them. Knowing that assures me that my family is beloved, just as it is. And so is yours. Surely this means we need not be anxious, not on this day, or any other one for that matter.

This week:

- What really does matter to you? How do these values shape your gratitude?
- What are some of your fondest memories of this day? Your most difficult ones? How was Jesus present in all of those times?
- How can you invite Jesus to join your celebration?
- How can you witness to Jesus in your celebration?

- How can you take Jesus to others today and on other days, too?
- What are you worried about today? How can you allow Jesus to ease your anxiety?